OFF HIGHWAY:
JOURNEYS OF NOVA SCOTIA WRITERS

Off Highway: Journeys of Nova Scotia Writers
Copyright ©2017
Stone Cellar Publications
Dartmouth, Nova Scotia

Stone Cellar Publications
ISBN-13: 978-0993833816
ISBN-10: 0993833810
October 2017

Edited by Sue Soares

Cover images by Judi Risser
Front cover: Boardwalk at Risser's Beach, Petite Riviere, NS
Back cover: Sperry's Beach, Petite Riviere, NS

APPRECIATION

We thank the Dartmouth Heritage Museum's Evergreen House and the Alderney Gate Branch, Halifax Regional Library, in whose pleasant meeting rooms we shared stories and made the many decisions leading to the publication of this volume. The resources provided by libraries and museums are deeply appreciated by writers everywhere.

CONTENTS

FOREWORD

This anthology of Nova Scotia authors is a collection of spirited prose and poetry written by a range of writers with diverse and intriguing backgrounds. Here you will find history, poetry, fiction and creative nonfiction by men and women who have been TV writers, animators, genealogists, teachers, playwrights, museum curators, scientists and more. Many of these writers have travelled far and wide but they have strong ties and a deep fondness for this province.

Each has been driven to record events and translate the meaning of those events into meaningful stories and poems to share with an audience well beyond their families.

First and foremost, each entry speaks some eternal truth about home: living in it, searching for it, finding it, losing it, going back to it. I came here as an immigrant myself in 1978 and, even though I did not grow up here, Nova Scotia felt like home from the first time I set foot on the sand and rocks of the province's shoreline. When we write of home in all its varied forms, we dig deep to attempt to speak of the passion we feel for the places we love and the things about those places that have shaped our unique identities and, indeed, understanding of our world.

The immigrants from the past and present come to life in these pages and we are again reminded that here in North America, we all came from somewhere else. Maybe not just us individually, but most certainly our ancestors have come from afar. We are all related and, deep down, none of us is much different from the next. We are connected. Always.

Telling stories helps to reconnect us to friends and strangers. We cherish our individual identity but tell our tales to let others know we have lived through events that shape us and unite us to each other, the past and the future.

This collection brings together ideas about choices we make in our lives and choices that are made for us. So many immigrants coming to Nova Scotia in the past came here because they had little choice. Forced for economic or political reasons, they arrived and made the best of it. For some, Nova Scotia and Canada was a safe haven and a place to begin again. For those like me, it was a place to create a life in a place that was new and exciting to me and welcoming as well.

There are stories of adventure here and travel. These writers have ranged far and wide across the planet. The days of sailing ships and youthful sailors shipping out of tiny Nova Scotia ports for foreign continents is long gone, but we still seem to be a peripatetic breed that needs to see what's out there on the farther shores before making our inevitable pilgrimage back home to the land of the Bluenose.

These writings tell about discoveries close to home and far away. And, in the telling of the tale and the shaping of a poem, we see the work of active, engaging minds taking the raw material of memory and shaping it into something meaningful, something revealing and illuminating.

Memory itself is evergreen. Experiences and our emotional attachment to those experiences remain alive and well through memory but through written language, the writer nails it down once and for all, gives it meaning and, by sharing the story, sets it free to go out into the world and have a literary life of its own.

Enjoy the journey out and the path back home.

Lesley Choyce
Lawrencetown Beach
August 6, 2017

OFF HIGHWAY:
JOURNEYS OF NOVA SCOTIA WRITERS

EVERGREEN WRITERS GROUP

OFF HIGHWAY
TOM ROBSON

Is Life a highway or is it a series of detours, some chosen, some enforced? There are life-changing detours that may be deliberately taken or accidental. Many take us, all too briefly, from that driving hardtop. Some of us seek far more of these than society endorses, making the detours life's journey.

A pause in the journey, a brief deviation.

St. Anne des Lacs. Mid-seventies. House party. Labatt's 50 stubby in hand. Singing along—if I know the words. Five guitars, all acoustic. Dying chords of one song prompt another. Nonstop music. Endless beers. Munchies. Smoke-filled room. One rule—if we want to smoke weed, do it outside; kids still run around in here!

Always some Lightfoot. "Carefree Highway." Too pensive. Too relaxed for a party mood. Can't blame just the music. Someone takes us in another direction with The Beatles' "Long and Winding Road."

Now the room and the stragglers who never left the kitchen are into it. Eddie is reminded of another sixties' hit that prolongs the road theme. We recognize the guitar intro and join in that journey down a long and winding road to the unknown.

And here we are, carrying our lightweight brothers—in unison. And that's the purpose of this detour. We're on a backroad, led by the Hollies, escaping in song.

But in our thirties, as I was then, most of us are on life's highway even if we're not sure it's what we want. We wonder if there isn't somewhere better and more meaningful and satisfying. "Am I in a rut?" is the secret question most of us ask ourselves.

To avoid answering, we escape on detours—frequent, but short— like the parties that help us avoid life and the highway's demands. Today, we collect toys and devices thought to be essential, but they only serve to distract and occupy our time.

We should know that life's drive along the highway is reminiscent of that unintentional meandering along the seventies Laurentian Autoroute in a snowstorm—before the ploughs have cleared a straight path. We know where the hardtop will take us, but it's a little more interesting weaving along on an unpredictable surface.

We may want to get off that highway, but sliding into a hazard isn't the preferred option. Yet some of life's travellers become unintentional deviators, while others deliberately leave the highway for who knows where.

I'm not sure at what age we realize that life is more than the highway we seem set on. When, if ever, do we know that we can't slip away from that highway? When we choose a highway journey through life, there is a danger that we are just carried along. At some stage, we begin to recall, with fondness, those parts of the journey that happened when we left the highway—the diversions.

A partner might agree to take these diversions. We may pleasantly recall those steps, sometimes deliberately taken and sometimes serendipitous, that carried us up or down a ramp onto a different route.

Marriage, moving, children, job change, losses, windfalls, relationship traumas, world events: the list of factors promoting deviance is endless and personal.

Our life may alter radically. Our journey may be steered in a different direction. Perhaps we escaped the mainstream, but the tributary we joined has many qualities like the route we left behind.

We think of life as a purposeful journey. Unfortunately, its purpose is beset by roadblocks that require us to take a detour or, sometimes, totally change direction. We, and our entourage, may plan for these and other excursions. Eventually, deviations, intended to be a time-out from the purpose, can become the purpose.

Such diversions are certainly part of retirement when we hope we've gotten off the high-speed highway. But know the journey is still ongoing for as long as we can navigate the quieter roads, perhaps to distant places.

Like me, we may still be looking for a party, one where we might spot a contemporary tuning up a six string, though his cigarette will no longer be lodged, smoking, between the strings, and the beer is more likely to be a glass of Merlot.

Whatever is sung, we will join in, though. If we ever knew the words, they're probably forgotten.

In the unlikely case that this event happens, I am going to google the lyrics to "You Can't Always Get What You Want" and memorize them. I'll ask my guitar buddy to play the necessary chords and, if I have to, I'll sing solo.

But I'll bet I'll be joined by those who know from where I'm coming in life's journey.

And after that, if I start "With a Little Help from my Friends" in my ageing imitation of Joe Cocker, we'll also agree on that aspect of the journey, and we'll travel in unison.

NEW BEGINNINGS

GOIN' UP THE ROAD
JANET McGINITY

This story is true, and events happened as described.
*You **can** go home again.*

A maple log crackled in the wood stove, sending off snaps and pops. Ice pearls melted and dripped off heavy sweaters and mittens hanging on a line behind the stove. The fragrance of wet wool and wood smoke filled the small kitchen. Our friend Bob passed around hot tea, spiked with Hennessey cognac that his father brought home from the Second World War, and which had stayed unopened in the wood shed ever since. The four of us sighed in silent contentment, enjoying the sweet, ancient cognac and the warmth of the stove door on our chilled toes.

My first husband, Brian, and I were spending part of a March Break holiday with old friends Roberta and Bob at Bob's family home near the village of Elgin, New Brunswick, in the hinterland of Albert County, across the river from Moncton. After supper and time getting reacquainted, Bob suggested we go tobogganing by starlight.

"Here's just the thing for making a toboggan go like snot," he said, holding up a can of Johnson's Floor Wax.

We waxed and polished the toboggans to a high gloss and headed out around ten o'clock to a nearby hill. Stars glittered under a new moon. The few houses along the road were dark and silent. Once we arrived, we coasted down the hill again and again, screaming and laughing, piling face first into the snow at the bottom until our skin reddened with cold. Around one o'clock in the morning, exhausted, we returned to the house.

Relaxing in a circle with our feet on the open wood stove door, we told stories of 'ghoulies and ghosties and long-leggity beasties, and things that go bump in the night.' I half-listened, with drooping eyelids. My shoulders ached pleasantly from the exercise. Around three o'clock, Bob banked the fire and we all went to bed.

The next day, the men built a new outhouse with the traditional crescent moon in the door, while Roberta and I peeled vegetables for soup and caught up on each other's lives. Both of us neared the end of university, unsure what to do next with our lives. In late afternoon, we regretfully waved goodbye.

"Wasn't that a great time?" I said to Brian as we drove to my parents' place in Moncton. "I miss Bob and Roberta so much. We'll have to come back this summer."

Back in Cambridge, Ontario, I thought often of the innocent fun we'd had that winter weekend. How comfortable I'd felt with these old friends, who I'd known since high school. How different that was compared to my life now. I was a student at the University of Waterloo but scarcely knew my classmates since I commuted daily and spent little leisure time on campus. I was also older, as I had restarted a stalled degree after several years' hiatus.

Something took root that winter weekend, seeded by a restlessness and longing that did not yet have a name.

A month or so later, Brian and I were invited to a party by one of his firefighter buddies in the suburban fire station where he worked. In my one good dress and high-heel shoes, I balanced a cocktail on my knee, making small talk with another firefighter's wife. She listened spellbound to the story I told. I thought, *Wow, I must be a great conversationalist.*

"Sounds like you enjoyed my story," I said to the woman.

"Well, the way you talk is so interesting," she replied. "You have quite an accent. Where did you say you're from? Somewhere Down East?"

I looked at her, crestfallen. Like many Maritimers, I drop my G's, pronounce 'house' as 'haouse' and 'boat' as "baout,' and express amazement with colourful phrases unknown to Ontarians. So, it was my accent that fascinated her—not what I was actually saying.

"Yes, I'm originally from Moncton," I replied. "I'm half Irish, half Acadian French. And you?"

"That's in um, Nova Scotia, isn't it? My grandparents came from somewhere in the States... I think."

This vagueness seemed strange, not knowing where her near ancestors came from. In Atlantic Canada, any chat with a stranger would start with "Where are you from?" or "Who's your father?" And in a half hour's chat, we always found a connection, whether it was mutual friends who went to the same school or a former neighbour from the same village. It made me feel like we were all part of the same extended clan—all we needed was to ask a few questions to see where we all fitted together.

The conversation with the firefighter's wife continued on the topic of current movies, none of which I'd seen, and gradually, we drifted away. I pondered that conversation on the way home. Roots didn't go deep here, I thought. Most people came from somewhere else. They, or their ancestors, made a clean break with the past when they started new lives after arriving from other parts of Canada, the United States, or Europe. They were no doubt nostalgic during the first few years but most only went back for occasional visits. Here, their concerns were their own, not that of their entire community of origin.

That wasn't a bad thing. Privacy was desirable, though carried to the extreme, it became isolation. Community could be carried to extremes, too. In the Maritimes, everyone knew everyone's business, and that was comforting when one needed help since one could ask a family member, friend, or neighbour, and he or she was generally willing. But if one never left, it was like a plant left too long in the same pot; one grew root bound. At some point, one needed to find fresh soil and more room to grow.

There had to be a balance between a need for privacy and being part of a community. I felt caught between the two.

By 1975, I had lived in Ontario for five years and assumed I'd spend the rest of my life there. I had left Moncton gladly, relieved to put miles between me and that grey city on its dirty chocolate-coloured river, its sticky heat in summer and its huge snowdrifts in winter. I knew every crack in every sidewalk. It was only a place to return to once or twice a year, for fleeting visits to family and school chums.

Now I saw a more nuanced picture. The friendships, close families, and relaxed pace of life Down East seemed more meaningful than the hurried, often shallow, social interactions we had in Ontario.

As winter turned into summer, Brian and I packed our camping gear for extended weekends away from Cambridge. Our favourite getaway was Lion's Head, a village on the Bruce Peninsula, part of a limestone escarpment that, on the map, looked like an elephant with the peninsula as its tail. We hiked parts of the Bruce Trail, did a little birdwatching and botanizing. On our way back to our campsite, we bought fresh-caught lake trout to grill over a charcoal fire.

On one of those long weekends, the same strange longing hit me, and I tried to figure it out. Finally, it dawned on me what it was. This Georgian Bay community could easily pass for a Maritime fishing village except for the rich iodine-laced odour of seaweed.

What I missed was the smell of the ocean.

Now I knew what was bothering me: I was homesick. I missed the Maritimes. But I couldn't just up stakes and move back. Brian had a job and family ties here. My graduation from the University of Waterloo was only months away, and I was determined to earn my degree.

My husband was an ex-Navy man who had been stationed in Halifax and liked the Maritimes. We had a heart-to-heart talk. He was open to the idea of leaving Ontario, as long as we both had good employment prospects. As a firefighter with a suburban station, he had little chance of promotion or challenge. He was restless.

One day in the winter of 1976, I stopped by the Cambridge public library to browse the magazines and saw an advertisement in *Nature Canada* for a community college program titled Historical/Natural Interpretation Services. The program had a prerequisite of a university degree.

This course taught students how to take scientific or historical information and present it in creative and interesting ways to the public. Skills learned were applicable to national parks and historic sites, science centres and zoos. A shiver of excitement went up my spine. I photocopied the article, raced home, and showed it to Brian.

"Wouldn't this be great? With a diploma from Seneca, I could maybe get a job with a national park in the Maritimes. What do you think?"

Intrigued, he did a little research and found that the school, Seneca College of Applied Arts and Technology in King City, Ontario, also offered a commercial diver program. Brian had learned to dive in the Navy and now saw a way of learning skills for a new career.

We contacted the school, and within a month, completed application forms for our respective programs. I arranged to graduate with a general degree in Psychology that spring, and Brian resigned from his firefighting job.

By September 1976, we were both enrolled at Seneca College. The school is on the former Eaton estate, the founders of the department store chain. I studied botany, zoology, biology, and photography and practiced presentation skills in front of fellow students. Brian attended the diving school, which used a fifty-acre lake as the practice site. We found student digs nearby, at a guest cottage on a hobby farm.

The school charged modest tuition fees, but in return, required each student to work a minimum of twenty hours a week on campus. The Eaton Castle, formerly the family's home, housed the cafeteria and offices. It often hosted conferences and wedding receptions in the

Great Hall. For my campus job, I worked in the cafeteria kitchen, preparing three hundred servings of Jell-O at a go and mashed potatoes by the bucket. (I still loathe Jell-O!). Brian and his fellow diving students waited tables and tended bar during special events at the castle.

The months flew by in an exhausting schedule of days that started at dawn and ended at seven or eight o'clock in the evening, often with a stop for takeout fish and chips in Newmarket.

Over the winter, I applied for a summer naturalist job at Fundy National Park, and Brian contacted several diving companies around Atlantic Canada. We both flew to Moncton for job interviews. Finally, in the spring of 1977, came the letters we had hoped for. Fundy National Park offered me a position as a national park interpreter, or naturalist. Brian got good news too: a job offer to join a dive team laying an electrical power cable on the sea floor of the Northumberland Strait between New Brunswick and Prince Edward Island. Work would start as soon as the ice was gone from the strait.

In late April, we packed the car with a few precious books and records, the remainder of our possessions, and headed for the Maritimes. The heady odour of seaweed was ambrosia in my nostrils as we cruised along the old coast road south through New Brunswick.

Over the previous ten months at Seneca, I had studied the ecological concept of habitat, that animals, plants, birds, and most other species had adapted to live in specific areas and didn't do well outside them. Brian and I had uprooted ourselves to live in Ontario. Now, we were being uprooted again, but to return to familiar soil. We were 'goin' home.'

THE LONG JOURNEY HOME
JANET DOLEMAN

After composing a brief synopsis of the family history for a scrapbook, my inspiration was to flesh out the family tree of names and dates into feelings, memories, and stories shared by the surviving children, who are now senior citizens. With names changed and fictionalized scenes to fill in the unknown gaps, this story shows how a real-life family reacted to tragedy and harsh circumstances, a reality for many who lived in that era. The descendants not only survived, but propagated in great number.

The birthday party was in full swing. Delores was glad she'd gone to the extra trouble of baking a cake, decorating the living room, and ordering in sandwich trays. The cake was a hit, only crumbs and smears of icing remained.

Her mother, Mabel, hadn't wanted her to order sandwiches. "Too expensive!" she insisted, but Delores overruled her mother's objections and watched from the background as her mother's attention had been completely hijacked by greeting the steady stream of friends and neighbours. She hadn't complained about the food once.

When the doorbell rang about fifteen minutes after the party began, revealing Mabel's sisters, Aunt Helena and Aunt Lulu from Nova Scotia, that was the real icing on the cake: a surprise that her mother would talk about for weeks and months to come. Imagine, traveling all that way for a birthday party! She could tell that she was more than pleased.

Delores surmised that there were only so many surprises left at the age of ninety. She doubted her mother would let a small thing like a ninetieth birthday slow her down. She was glad her two aunts had decided to come; they were not young either, and it was a long way to travel. Of the eight siblings, only four were left. After hearing stories from her mother's childhood here and there over the years, it meant that this time together was doubly precious.

As she moved in and out of the room, clearing plates and debris, she heard snatches of conversation from the three sisters, the "girls" they called themselves. Not wanting to disturb their time together, she hovered closer.

"Do you remember...?"

"Did you see so-and-so's obituary?"

"I still can't believe we made it all that way."

This last remark referred not to their recent flight from Halifax, but an arduous journey across the country long ago.

***

Mabel, Helena, and Lulu's father had been a barber, plying his trade wherever he could find work, finding small successes that repeatedly turned out badly. He'd served in the Army out of Winnipeg, married their mother Maureen, and moved their young family repeatedly from town to town in western Canada and in the Pacific Northwest. They eventually travelled across the country to the East Coast, where their father had grown up.

Delores recalled photographs but never knew her grandparents, who had been caught up in a series of tragedies, not least of which was the economic collapse leading to the Great Depression. The horror stories and images of people jumping from tall buildings in New York and Chicago seemed detached and remote. What was only too real for them were the abandoned farms of the Prairies, dirt blowing away in great sifting clouds and whorls of dust. Their shoes wore thin enough to feel rocks right through them. They stuffed folded pieces of cardboard inside to cover the soles and make them last a little longer. Her mother liked to tell her how she'd learned to turn shirt collars and still practiced it. She also enjoyed the adventure of exploring second-hand shops, searching for that elusive good quality garment for next to nothing.

"People don't realize how rich they are," she'd say. "Look at how easily they throw out perfectly good clothes!"

Her grandparents must have been made of pretty tough stock to have travelled the rough roads of British Columbia and Alberta back in those days with a carload of children and perhaps all their worldly possessions. In the 1920s and 1930s, want ads were scarce, attracting long lines of out-of-work men. Even though her mother had been very young, she'd tell the story of the whole family piling into Father's big car to travel to yet another town. Other families camped in the rough along the roadsides, tucked behind scant groves of trees for privacy. Two or three families would group together for protection, wary of vagrants roaming the roads. Their father's old car used to break down every few miles, it seemed. They had to climb out and make do with going in the bushes to relieve themselves while he tinkered with the engine. Their mother took those opportunities to rummage amongst the boxes and sacks of food to assemble a makeshift lunch. Sacks of potatoes were tied to the running boards, and boxes were strapped to the trunk.

It was those cold nights, bundled in blankets and sleeping under a tarp, that she would recall distastefully when someone suggested going on a camping trip.

"Show me the RV!" she'd say loudly. Mabel's favourite method of "camping" was pulling up to a motel room door.

Delores had been curious to see the family records listing the birthdates and birthplaces of her mother's siblings; a handful of yellowed paper documents were kept in an envelope in the china cabinet. Careful study and simple math indicated to her that every new town meant that another baby was on the way. Her mom was a little vague about the traveling, but when Aunt Gertrude visited two or three times a year, she did not hesitate to share juicy stories. Being the eldest sibling, she had the best memory, or so she said. She'd also died the earliest, at sixty-nine.

One story was so vivid it gave Delores nightmares. The family had been driving through the mountains during a violent rainstorm. Rain drumming on the roof, wind buffeting the car, when Father could drive no farther because of a rockslide blocking the road ahead.

"What did you do?' she remembered asking. "How did you get out of there?"

"We slept in the car that night, or tried to," explained Aunt Gertrude. "We couldn't see anything. It was so black and much too dangerous to risk turning around. I must have fallen asleep, as squashed as we were with the suitcases and stuffed flour sacks piled around our heads, like sardines in a can. The next thing I remember, it was light outside and a man was hitching a rope from his truck to the front bumper and hauling us through a cleared path in the road."

Every chance she got, Delores asked Aunt Gertrude to tell her more. She would hang around the house as close by as possible without appearing too obvious, although Mabel was adamant about sending children outdoors to play if the weather was decent. Delores soon found out that some stories were not meant for children's ears, which made them all that more attractive. It was then that their voices lowered, and Delores strained to hear from the hallway. Occasionally, she hid behind the thick drapes, trying not to sneeze, wishing she'd brought paper and pencil to write down every word.

One day, while hidden from view, she was surprised to hear sniffles coming from the sofa. Was it Aunt Gertrude or her own mother who hardly ever cried? They'd been talking about their mother, Delores' grandmother, and how sick she'd been while pregnant with the last child, her Uncle James.

"I can't imagine how she managed to look after us, now that I've raised my own children, and her alone and ill. Father died that spring. It was horrible. She was so sick that the neighbour ladies came with pots of stew and biscuits for dinner, and we felt like animals in a zoo. Don't you remember it was right after that the doctor came and ordered Mother into the hospital? Mrs. Johnston next door moved in with us for a while to cook and clean. She wasn't so bad, but then she went away, and we had to pack little bags for the orphanage."

Her mother spoke then, sniffling a bit. It *had* been her crying.

"I do remember that day, how frazzled Dorothy was trying to get us organized, the boys refusing to find their shoes, and how we left the house in such a hurry. For some reason, I can't recall the faces of the people who took us there, but I will never, ever forget my first sight of that huge brick building." This was when the family was living in Winnipeg, and the brick building was St. Bartholomew's. Aunt Gertrude spoke again, in a hushed tone.

"Dorothy got up one night to use the bathroom, and when she got back to bed, she told me what she overheard in the hallway. Two of the nursing sisters were talking, and she heard them say, 'Why doesn't she hurry up and die, so we can get rid of these children?' Dorothy's face was as white as a sheet, and she shivered the rest of the night. I know because we shared a bed in that dormitory."

Delores could hardly believe her ears, and as hard as she tried, she couldn't erase those terrible words from her thoughts, even all these years later. Her mother and aunts seemed so happy now, as if their traumatic childhood had happened to someone else. They survived the orphanage; in fact, Aunt Helena remembered being given a doll with curly hair and blinking eyes for Christmas. During their stay, their mother delivered her last child and died of cancer short months later.

The children were now orphans and had to endure being shunted back and forth between Winnipeg and Nova Scotia while the Social Service authorities decided who was responsible for them. Relatives in

Nova Scotia would have taken two or three, but no one wanted or was able to take all eight. The baby was colicky, crying and crying, which didn't help their case. Dorothy and Gertrude, the two eldest, used to take turns rocking him and walking the hallways to comfort him. *You'd never know it now,* thought Delores, thinking of her Uncle James' quiet nature.

She'd heard about the train journeys, snippets from Aunt Gertrude and the uncles when they visited. Travelling by train sounded romantic, but their experience must have been the total opposite. Eight of them crammed onto wooden benches, with no proper place to sleep, and their basket of food depleted long before they reached their destination. Aunt Gertrude, "the outspoken one," she'd called herself, told everyone about the first time she'd spoken to a black man, who was a porter on the train.

"I couldn't stop staring at his face, which was more brown than black," she'd said. "He was always so courteous and polite, and made sure we had water to drink. He used to produce all kinds of things from his pockets: dinner rolls and treats wrapped in white napkins from the dining car, bottles of root beer for the boys."

"I remember the smelly toilet at the end of the rail car," said her mother. "I might have been too young to remember much, but I will never forget that! Dorothy was appalled, but we had to make do the best we could."

While listening to the three sisters reminisce, Delores wiped the tabletop and tidied the array of bright birthday cards on the mantelpiece. Her thoughts strayed to the other siblings and her cousins, all of whom were descendants of the man and woman who had died so suddenly, and tragically young. People hearing their story shook their heads in amazement and disbelief that these eight children not only survived but thrived and lived productive lives.

Their mother had made them all promise they would not give up their family name and that they were not to be adopted. Despite being dispersed to foster homes, they lived in close proximity and kept in touch with each other, the two eldest girls keeping an eye out for the younger brothers and sisters. Three joined the Canadian military, all of them married and raised families, ran businesses, or were teachers. Later in life, four siblings embarked on a trip to British Columbia and Alberta to retrace portions of their parents' journey.

Every summer, a family reunion picnic or lobster boil was held at an old farmhouse near the coast of Nova Scotia, becoming a tradition for as many as could get there. The yearly gatherings helped them establish deeper sibling ties, unearthing fragments of stories from childhood that the younger ones hadn't heard. Aunt Lulu was only three when her parents died and got to know her siblings only after she was married.

Delores knelt to retrieve a black leather photo album from the bookcase in the hallway. She leafed through the pages until she found what she was looking for. The faded photograph was now one hundred years old, a man in uniform standing straight, shoulders back, puttees and boots together, buttons polished, cap set so the bill partially obscured his eyes, staring back at the camera.

"My son bears some resemblance to this image from 1915, although the eyes are shaded by the cap." The caption below read *Llewellyn Heywood Williamson served in the Canadian Army out of Winnipeg, married Maureen in 1918 and fathered eight children.* A short sixteen years later, he died suddenly, plunging his wife and children into a state of chaos and peril. They were at the mercy of the era and of well-meaning relatives and, eventually, the state.

This is not my story to tell, thought Delores, *but maybe it is, because here I am caught up in the long thread of stories, memories, and events that filters down through the timeline to my generation and to my children's. It would be wonderful to have known him and my grandmother, to tell them about our family, which has grown and spread across this country, even back to where their little family began.*

That night, exhausted from the party aftermath, she fell asleep and dreamt she was on a train…

She felt her eyelids grow heavy and fought to keep herself awake. The uneven rhythm, the intermittent screech of iron wheels on rails, rattling, whistles and bells at the crossings—each sound registered in a level of consciousness beyond the present, bringing her to the brink of being awake. Then, a slipping back, down into a hazy semi-aware state. She could see the boys across from her, George age twelve with his arm around Howard, both dozing while leaning against each other. Howard, whose grubby little face was streaked with tears, clutched a blanket in his chubby fist, a remnant of blue cloth worn thin by repeated rubbing of small thumbs. She wondered how she was going to get them cleaned up before they arrived in Halifax. Would anyone be there to meet them? And who was going to want us?

FROM THE PHILANTHROPIC
TOM ROBSON

There are three stories of life journeys here. They are joined by a common thread, the Royal Philanthropic Society, which is, in itself, a fourth story.

A group of well-to-do men of influence met in the fashionable St. Paul's Coffee House in London in 1788, forming "The Philanthropic Society." They had no idea they were planting the seed for life-changing journeys from the institution they were in the process of establishing. The destination of some who made the journey was Nova Scotia.

The Society's announced purpose was "to help young people caught up in crime to develop virtuous dispositions and industrious habits, and, ultimately find them the means of honest employment and livelihood." To these ends, they financed a rescue mission. In 1832, their reformatory was transferred from inner London's St. Georges Fields to a farm at Redhill, thirty miles south in the Surrey countryside. Guilty children, once automatically committed to adult prisons, could be diverted to serve time at The Philanthropic Society's Reformatory.

At the farm, they could learn skills and work habits they could employ on their release. But these skills and knowledge weren't always suited to inner city life from which most of the boys originated. Placing them back into that environment was, the Society believed, a recipe for a return to crime. They argued it would be better to ship them off to the colonies where there were opportunities. One of these colonies was Nova Scotia.

In January 1967, I joined the staff at The Royal Philanthropic Society's Approved School. As its then title implied, it was a changed institution, which continued to help delinquent youth. It was still supported, in part, by the Society but was just one of a nationwide chain of Home Office residential schools approved for the treatment of delinquents ordered there by juvenile courts. It still had its working farm and some residential homes for youth aged fifteen and over, who could spend up to three years there. It also had a secure unit for some who persisted in running away and re-offended while absconding.

I was a teacher/housemaster and, later, administrator in the third Redhill component. The "Classifying School" received newly sentenced delinquents, aged ten to sixteen, for a minimum of three weeks social, educational, psychiatric, psychological, behavioural, and family assessment. This intensive and comprehensive process determined which of the many residential approved schools in England could best meet the recommendations of the treatment plan the assessment produced.

Almost a thousand boys passed through this classification procedure in each of my five years there. Out of necessity the staff learned and adapted more quickly than their clients. We lived at the school and worked extra evenings, overnights, and weekends. There was constant pressure to complete assessments, compile reports, and move the boys on to a treatment facility. My years there were possibly the most fruitful of my working life. But not the most enjoyable.

During my five years at "The Philanthropic" in Redhill, I became interested in its history and spent many hours reading annual reports and client records. These dated back to the 1700s, gathering dust in the attic of the original warden's house. Many years later, living in Nova Scotia, I learned that some of the "Home Children" brought here and placed with families, under the patronage and guidance of Colonel Laurie of Oakfield, were emigrants sent from The Philanthropic. I wondered if comparing my journey with that of the immigrant youth one hundred years previously would make an interesting story.

After the institution's closure, the Society's client records were put in the care of the Surrey County History Centre. The collection features a register of admissions from 1788 to 1906. The original records of these inmates had been preserved and were accessible.

From the register, I gleaned a list of forty who were discharged from Redhill to Nova Scotia approximately a hundred years prior to my own journey. I randomly selected two Philanthropic emigrants who were sent on that journey. I applied for copies of their Philanthropic histories. These became source material for the following stories. Accessing the copperplate handwritten records made fascinating reading though their accuracy cannot be confirmed and details are sparse.

William Lee. Emigrated to Nova Scotia in 1874.

William Lee could barely see over the barrier that surrounded the prisoner's dock in Godstone courthouse. He looked around the room for an aunt or uncle, hoping that one of them would offer help or, better still, a home. But the only familiar face he saw at his trial that morning of the twenty-first of November, 1870, was that of the Master of Bletchingley Union Workhouse. The young orphan knew that no help was coming from that direction.

He had only sneaked into that garden and stolen carrots because he was hungry. Theft of the carrots was the charge. Perhaps he shouldn't have run away from work at Mr. Smith's stables. Every workplace to which the workhouse master sent him was worse than the last. Sleeping in a barn in November wasn't what he wanted. And the food wasn't much better than that offered to the horses and hogs. He was only small, but he needed more food than Mr. Smith provided if he was to grow. He wasn't sure how old he was—maybe thirteen—probably older. His aunt and uncles could never agree on that. Whatever his age, William was small.

His attention was drawn back to the evidence being given to the magistrates by the Workhouse Master.

"Both parents died before this boy was ten. Neither aunts nor uncles can provide a home. Many situations have been procured but nobody, not even his family, can keep him because of his lazy and dishonest habits and want of truthfulness. Several punishments have failed to bring about a change in attitude. The theft of the carrots occurred on his latest escape from honest work. The Union Workhouse can offer no more to this youth."

When asked if he had anything to say, William promised he would change and stay wherever he was sent. He told the magistrates that this was the first time he had ever stolen and hoped they wouldn't send him to prison like that other time when he had been arrested for vagrancy.

His pleas were wasted.

The chief magistrate, Lord Cottenham, ordered William to serve fourteen days in the Wandsworth House of Corrections. After this, he would serve five years at The Philanthropic Society's Reformatory at Redhill. William knew this was only minutes away from both the courthouse and William's home village of Bletchingley, thirty miles into the Surrey countryside from London. But he was taken to prison in London anyway.

Two weeks later, William Lee returned to spend the next three and a half years working the farm at the Redhill Reformatory where he was a member of Gurney's House. In that residence, he was supervised and disciplined by the housemaster and his wife, the matron. On admission, this redhead, who had briefly attended elementary school in Redhill and at the Bletchingley Union, couldn't read, write, or 'cypher.' He must have acquired some reading and writing skill while at The Philanthropic.

The rare occasions when he committed petty infractions against the rules are the only records of this lengthy episode in this young man's life. The worst punishment was three days in a cell for stealing sixpence. William would have gained some skills, work habits, self-discipline, and knowledge of farming. He never ran away but there is no record of contact with his relatives, all of whom lived within five miles from The Philanthropic. In the 1871 British census, he was recorded as a sixteen-year-old living at the Redhill Reformatory.

The question became what to do with this reformed offender as he approached adulthood. None of his three uncles and an aunt were willing, or able, to offer a home, if indeed they were asked. An older brother had enlisted in the army and there is no record of other siblings.

The Philanthropic Society, from its inception in 1788, had been a progressive organization concerned with the aftercare of those it had helped. What was to be done with those who had been reformed in their lengthy stay at The Philanthropic? Returning them to the mean streets, an unsupportive environment and an oftentimes criminally inclined family was counter-productive. One answer was for them to emigrate to the colonies. The Philanthropic Society wasn't the only organization to pursue this aftercare policy. It persisted for more than two hundred years, placing vagrant and orphan children as well as delinquents with families in South Africa, Australia, and Canada. It is a program that has been widely condemned because of frequent abuse of the Home Children and denial of their opportunity to return to family—whatever its circumstances. Yet it is estimated that one in six of today's Canadian population is related to a Home Child.

Even though William wasn't from an inner-city slum, he became a Home Child. The minimal records of the 1870s Philanthropic simply note, "Fifteenth of June, 1874, emigrated to Nova Scotia."

The passenger list of the Steamship *Prussian*, arriving at Quebec City from Liverpool via Londonderry on the eleventh of May, 1874 included a Chas. W. N. Lee, born about 1853, arriving with a large group of young people, almost certainly immigrant Home Children. William was listed as twenty-one though he could have been up to four years younger according to Philanthropic and later census records. Much of his early life is a mystery. There is no record of a William Lee landing in Halifax in 1874. Perhaps he did travel somehow from Quebec City to Nova Scotia.

He had spent his previous four years within five miles of his birthplace and neglectful relatives on familiar farmland, in a strict, controlled environment where work ethic was paramount and his future was in the hands of those into whose care he had been confined by the court. He was then put in the care of strangers on the train journey to London and then to Liverpool for a trans-Atlantic voyage to he knew not what or where.

Where would he live? With whom and how? These questions would be answered by whichever colonist continued the philanthropic endeavours of finding home, work, and a future for these Home Children. William Lee was one of the fortunates. He was taken in by Colonel Laurie, housed and employed on his estate at Oakfield, Nova Scotia, from 1874 until after 1901.

There were three sparse reports recorded back at The Philanthropic School by the fall of 1875. Each reported that William was "doing well at Colonel Laurie's." The next year, William himself wrote to a Mr. Best, housemaster at Redhill, that he was "doing well." The rest of his message is unclear. In 1877, it was again recorded that he was "doing well."

In November 1877, he married Margaret Busteed. She was from Londonderry. But whether she was an immigrant from the Irish city, as her name suggests, or a nineteen-year-old resident of the small farming community of the same name a few miles north of Oakfield, is unclear. This marriage was the last notation on William's record at The Philanthropic. Five years after the event, on the tenth of August, 1882, it is recorded that William is "married and working for Colonel Laurie. Has done well. A hardworking, honest fellow."

William and Margaret had six children: Libby or Lilly, William, Robert, George, Hamilton or Harton, and Marsden. After the 1901 census, the family moved or dispersed. Some are in the 1911 census, but no longer at Oakfield. William and his wife, with three sons, were somewhere in the Fall River/Beaverbank area. The search for them continues. Their descendants may still be around. Do they know the story of their "Home Child" ancestor?

George Bishop. Sent to Nova Scotia in 1862.

George came to Nova Scotia and returned to his home in London around the time that William Lee was orphaned. George was an early Home Child, sent to what was to become Canada even before the reception, placement, and support network was reliably established. He didn't stay.

In character and background, George contrasts with William. His birthdate, the fifth of April, 1845, is unquestioned. He was the oldest of three sons of George and Maryanne Bishop, born in Plaistow, inner London. There was also a sister some twelve years younger. The parents moved with George to nearby Lambeth and then to Vauxhall Walk. George was raised in the city but found his way, courtesy of the magistrates, to The Philanthropic Reformatory's Farm in the Surrey countryside shortly after his fourteenth birthday.

Unlike first-offender William Lee, George, with the reported encouragement of his father, was a career thief. Before he was fourteen, he had been found guilty and jailed on eight occasions. He had been sentenced to seven three-month terms in adult jail, plus a week for breaking a window. He could count himself lucky that at his ninth trial on the first of November, 1858, he was sent from the Clerkenwell Sessions Court to serve six months' imprisonment at the Westminster House of Corrections.

Why lucky? Rather than being given a much longer prison sentence in an adult jail, the rest of George's punishment was four years' detention at The Philanthropic Reformatory in Redhill. His "good and anxious mother" must have been relieved.

There are two ironies around his offence. The charge was "stealing a skittle ball." We will never know why or what he needed it for. Previous thefts were of money or clothing to sell. George was a thief and a pickpocket—but stealing the wooden equivalent of a bowling ball makes little sense.

The site where George served his prison sentence is now occupied by Westminster Cathedral. The Westminster House of Corrections, a forbidding, dark, and ancient building in Victorian times, was pulled down some years after George's transfer to Redhill Reformatory on the thirtieth of April, 1859. At The Philanthropic farm, the only walls and fences were to keep the livestock penned.

The recorded description of George, on admission, seems at odds with his criminal history. He wasn't a threatening, prematurely mature brute. George was only four feet seven inches tall, had a "dark, swarthy complexion, dark brown hair, dark eyes, and a straight, sharp nose." Though his figure was "slight," he was "well-made and compact." His "bullet head" was noted, as was a "clear, good eye and long eyelashes." The final descriptor was "determined looking." He was less a "Bill Sykes" and more of an "Artful Dodger."

Between thieving, he had worked with his father as an "iron moulder" and then as a painter. There had been some schooling at the National School at Clerkenwell and George was said to read "fairly" but "write and cypher very little." His general ability was described as "good."

Remarkably, George stayed at The Philanthropic Society's Reformatory for three full years. The inner-city urchin settled in the country, and there are no reports of him running back to London. There were seventeen notations of misbehaviour in those three years, mostly for avoiding work or minor infractions such as "making a noise in the bedroom," for which he was "caned," or "singing about the house."

In July 1861, he was allowed home on leave for three days, and he returned on time. The following April, he returned to Redhill from another three-day leave. On that occasion, he probably knew that he would soon be shipped off to Canada. The prospect must have become acceptable because he left his family, knowing that he might never see them again. But in January, it had been recorded that George had been put in a cell for three days for "disorderly and violent conduct." Speculation could conclude that this was his reaction to being informed that he was being sent to Canada instead of going home to Lambeth.

For 1862, the next note in his file reads, "Twenty-ninth of April, Emigrated to Canada per Nova Scotian."

The steamship *Nova Scotian* plied between Liverpool and Saint John, New Brunswick, and Halifax. Where this eighteen-year-old immigrant disembarked is unknown, but in all probability it was Halifax. With whom he was placed, where, and in what working capacity is unknown. The only record we have of him in this country is in The Philanthropic Reformatory's file: "Ninth of September, 1862. Returned to London, gives a false account of his treatment in Canada."

What had happened? Did he lie to arrange removal from his new abode? Did he manipulate a passage back across the Atlantic in just five months? How did he do that? Did the receiving agent find his attitude impossible to accommodate? Did he quickly fall foul of the colonial law and get himself deported? Was he, perhaps, one of those "Home Children" who was abused or exploited?

This immigrant's stay was brief. His move to the colonies was unsuccessful. The September 1862 report said that George had worked at a pie shop on Union Street in London, but left. By the twenty-first of October, he had walked into a hatters and departed with fifteen hats. He had reverted to his criminal acts and was committed for trial. On the seventeenth of November, he was sentenced to four years' penal servitude. He was eighteen years old and less than three months back in London.

What had happened to George was what organizations such as The Philanthropic Society feared. If children, diverted from possible prison sentences and placed in homes or reformatories, were sent back to their families and former neighbourhoods, they were at risk of reverting to criminal behaviours.

It seemed that George was destined for a life in jail. Either emigration had been mishandled, or he had rejected the new life and manipulated his return to London.

But there is a happy ending. George served all four years of his final, recorded jail sentence. Back at home in November, he found work at an iron foundry. In February 1867, his father reported that after George was laid off, he enlisted in the Green Jackets regiment of the army, 4th battalion, 60th rifles, The King's Royal Rifle Corps.

George left the army after another four years, on the fifteenth of July, 1871. The following year, he visited The Philanthropic Reformatory. He was then "in the army reserve, intending to join the band for which he practises religiously. This earns him four shillings a day. In addition, he earns twenty-four shillings a week as a painter's labourer at J.W. Ironside, coach makers."

Remarkably, George had turned his life around.

Fourteen years passed. On the third of August, 1886, the forty-one-year-old George Bishop again journeyed from Lambeth down to The Philanthropic at Redhill. George's repeated visits to The Philanthropic indicate that his stay there had meaning for him—perhaps the meaning of "an old home." The final note on his file reads, "Visits School. Very respectable wholesale and retail confectioner in partnership with his brother at eighty-four, Fryer Street, Lambeth."

George Bishop had been sentenced to prison nine times before he was fifteen. He'd then spent three years detained at The Philanthropic Society's Reformatory. He made a quick emigrant journey to Nova Scotia, didn't like what he found, and came back to a life of crime. At age twenty-one, he was released from another four-year jail sentence. Yet, twenty years later, he is an upstanding citizen of Lambeth, running a candy store.

Tom Robson. Emigrated from The Philanthropic in 1971.

One hundred years later, in the 1970s I, too, made the emigrant journey, eventually arriving in Nova Scotia. I had only two things in common with William and George. I had lived, worked, and learned at The Philanthropic "reformatory" for many years and I emigrated from The Philanthropic. Unlike George Bishop, I stayed. My history pales into insignificance when compared with the stories of those two who made the trip a century, or so, earlier.

My trek to Nova Scotia began one spring Friday coffee break in 1971 when a fellow worker at the Classifying School read aloud an advertisement from *The Times Educational Supplement*. It was recruiting Approved School personnel who had experience working with delinquents in a residential treatment setting. That evening, at least four of us wrote off for details of the opportunity to leave The Philanthropic and the country. The opportunity was in Canada, but we all believed that our years at The Philanthropic had prepared us for any challenge, anywhere.

In those pre-computer days, negotiating for a job abroad was a drawn-out process. Two of us pursued the opportunity, were interviewed, and were offered positions. Thanks to the work at The Philanthropic, I was deemed to be a specialist, an expert in my field. When decision day came, I was the only one who opted to become a landed immigrant, eligible to work in Canada. The situation was in Quebec.

In contrast to William and George, I was no callow youth being pushed into an alien situation. I wasn't a Home Child. I was a thirty-five-year-old husband and father of three, emigrating with an apprehensive, excited family and parental blessing. There was no trans-ocean passage in steerage—Liverpool to Montreal or Halifax. Sponsored immigrants flew from Heathrow in a jumbo jet. My valued skill and experience put me in this category, and my new employers booked and paid for our subsidised flight in December of 1971.

We landed in a snowstorm and were cautiously driven sixty kilometres north from Montreal to our rented Laurentian house, a comfortable distance from the campus at The Boys' Farm and Training School, Shawbridge, another facility intended to reform juvenile delinquents.

In total, I worked nine and a half years helping to determine treatment needs of delinquent youth before switching to a situation where I was the treatment agent. The truth is that it is easier to prescribe treatment than to administer it. In my final half year of my ten years working with confused, rebellious, delinquent, and troubled young persons, I burnt out.

On arrival in Canada, I was still more than seven years away from Nova Scotia. Much more happened in those years. I went back to teaching, still with special needs children, but they were no longer my responsibility after they left school each day for home. This change was too late to rescue a marriage and prevent my children moving to Ontario with their mother. I earned the degree that the English school system had determined I wasn't a candidate for some twenty years previously. My life in the "colonies" changed me.

My new wife and I determined that we needed to escape from the linguistic and political schizophrenia we felt as Anglophones in La Belle Province. To achieve this, I applied to work, again with delinquents, this time with teen girls in Nova Scotia. Fortunately, I was rejected. But I established contacts in the Nova Scotia school system, and in August of 1979, this now Canadian citizen settled beside the ocean in rural Nova Scotia and re-embarked on an interrupted journey of teaching "normal" children in "regular" school situations.

My five years at The Philanthropic had earned me my immigrant status. Thirty-six years, eight dwellings, and one Nova Scotia-born daughter later, we are still here and intend to stay. The 1788 philanthropists would see that I, like William and George, "developed a virtuous disposition and industrious habits and have found honest means of employment and livelihood."

In 1986, The Royal Philanthropic Society's School at Redhill closed. The Society still exists and continues to fund programs for disadvantaged young people.

I journeyed to Canada from an institution that was known for over a hundred years as The Philanthropic. I came willingly and, had I not enjoyed my new country, I could have returned to England. A hundred years before, the two Home Children making that journey in this story had little choice. Two of us settled in Nova Scotia. The third enterprising youth cheated the system, or did he?

LUNENBURG HOMECOMING
FRANK LEAMAN

*This story is part of a much longer piece I plan to write. It is
based on the real-life story of my father's father when he came
to Lunenburg, Nova Scotia. Some elements from other events
have been incorporated as well.*

The screeching of the parrot in the centre of the market square
competed with Consuela's shrieking. Emmanuel looked to see where it
sat in the palm tree as the hot sun beat down on the teenagers
standing around Consuela.

He barely remembered when his family had money, when the
Spanish still ruled San Juan. But now, the Americans were in charge,
and his parents hadn't survived the invasion. Emmanuel and his older
brother Angelo had found refuge on the streets of San Juan with other
orphaned children and youths. Consuela was their leader, and Angelo
was his protector. One day, Angelo disappeared from the streets. "He is
on a ship. He is gone," was all Emmanuel knew. Angelo had left without
saying goodbye.

Consuela spat on the pavement. This drew Emmanuel's attention
back to the present. Consuela's jet-black hair and gold earrings
glistened in the sun. She'd finished giving her orders for today. The
tray of cakes he held was to be sold by the time her spit dried.

When Angelo disappeared, Emmanuel was left alone to do
Consuela's bidding. He lived in fear because Consuela was a fearsome
creature, especially when she gave them their work for the day.

On this day, he made his way down to San Juan's harbour. There,
the sailors, who had been labouring for hours already, paused to buy
his cakes.

A schooner lay against the pier. She was black with a gold stripe on
either side. This two-masted vessel was called the Glendora Knickle.

Emmanuel watched from the shadows of the old warehouses as the crew of the Glendora toiled. They didn't seem like heathens. Rather, they were men who did their work in a jovial way. He watched three men joke with each other while they strapped cargo barrels in place on the deck.

Then he saw another man with a white beard come onto the deck to speak with his crew. The men showed deference for this man they called Captain Knickle. So this was the captain of the Glendora.

Emanuel decided he would cast his life into their world. "Ojalah," the Spanish word for hopefully, was all he could think.

Later, he watched as the crew walked up from the dock. This was their last night to party before the ship would leave San Juan.

At dusk, he slipped aboard and found a place between the barrels. With barrels to his left and barrels to his right, he felt snug and safely hidden from the men—and from Consuela. He soon fell asleep.

Before dawn, he woke as the big schooner moved towards the open sea. Through the gap in the ship rail, he watched the fortress San Felipe del Morro, as the ship passed it by, and until it disappeared below the horizon.

A crew member spotted Emmanuel.

"By the lightning twist!" the man exclaimed. "Why, muchacho benaki, pronto ondalay! Wait 'til the Old Man sees you!"

Emmanuel didn't understand all the words this muscled giant spoke. But he knew enough. He crawled out of his hiding spot.

The man took hold of his arm and marched him aft.

The following fifteen-minute meeting was the scariest time of his young life. Emmanuel stood tall, afraid of what his fate would be. But he remembered his friends saying, "Behind the mountains are more mountains."

He had chosen his course. Now he stood as if before King Solomon, waiting for his judgement! And knew there would be no appeal after he gave his decision.

"Do you speak English?" Captain Knickle asked, in Spanish.

"A little," Emmanuel told him.

"How old are you?"

"Fourteen years old."

The captain raised his brow. Did he not believe him?

"You look older," the man said. "Does your family know you came onto my ship?"

"My parents are dead."

Emmanuel looked older than his fourteen years from his hard life on the streets of San Juan. Captain Knickle saw a handsome youth who had dealt with things no young man of his age should have to. He saw that Emmanuel deserved a new opportunity.

The captain put the boy in the charge of the man who had found him hiding on the deck, the second mate, Mr. Mosher.

Mr. Mosher saw Emmanuel was hungry. He took him below to the fo'c's'le, sat him at the table, and told the cook, "Give the boy some cookies and a big mug of hot cocoa."

While Emmanuel ate and Mr. Mosher rummaged in a trunk, the cook busied himself preparing the noontime meal. He paused to ask why the boy was staring at him.

"Look at the wealth of food you have," Emmanuel said.

"You'll eat well, lad," Mr. Mosher said. "This cook might not be from Lunenburg, but he knows how to cook. What's for dinner today? As if we have a choice when it comes to what we get to eat!"

"Sauerkraut and Solomon Gundy," the man grunted as he pulled a crock from the cupboard.

"Good Lunenburg food!"

Mr. Mosher assigned Emmanuel a bunk, one close to the stove, and soon gave him warm clothes and raingear. The lad looked at the heavy clothes. Their destination was Lunenburg, Nova Scotia, Canada. This was their last run of the season. His imagination told him to prepare for a cold country.

Now, the second mate was taught that every man is a father to every child. Emmanuel sensed this in him. He felt at ease as the mate taught him rope and boat work.

He looked at this big man from Lunenburg in wonder and awe.

And soon, Emmanuel learned so much more.

He learned who held the authority in what aspects of the workings of the ship. Captain Knickle was always shown deference.

And quirks of the crew could be overlooked as the men worked together. Emmanuel was aware of Mr. Mosher's frequent visits to the spot between the barrels where he had discovered Emmanuel as they left San Juan. And he ignored, as the rest of the crew did, the smell of rum on Mr. Mosher's breath when he came back to work.

In the kitchen, the cook was in charge. He decided the meals. Generous portions of strange foods were dished out at every meal.

Mr. Mosher kindly helped by explaining what was in tongues and sounds, sauerkraut, house baking, boiled dinner, finnan haddie, and whatever else filled Emmanuel's plate. It took time for Emmanuel to enjoy the new tastes.

The cook, like Emmanuel, was different from the rest of the crew. He wasn't from Lunenburg, but from a village known as Peggy's Cove. And like Emmanuel, he went to sea to get away from hardship at home. The sailors told tales of battles the cook had with his wife, none of which the cook denied. He said that he went to sea to get away from his wife.

Eventually, Emmanuel felt less the Spanish colonial.

Things now progressed with Emmanuel until an event caused another unseen force to enter the picture. The first mate told Mr. Mosher to take Emmanuel with him on the late-night watch at the wheel to observe and learn. It was fair sailing, so Mr. Mosher, as was his custom on fair evenings like this, treated himself to a nip or two of the Glendora's cargo.

One of the deadly attributes of alcohol is it fools the drinker into thinking they know its power and that they can handle it.

In the late hours of the watch, Mr. Mosher fell asleep at the wheel! Emmanuel took the wheel and used his lessons to steer. In the dark of night, a monster appeared. What looked like an abandoned hulk of a ship wasn't far off their bow.

"Mr. Mosher, what is that?"

Mr. Mosher didn't answer. He had passed out.

Emmanuel knew something must be done now.

Emmanuel jumped on the man. He slapped him. He yelled in his ears.

He grabbed hold of the wheel again and turned with all his strength. Mr. Mosher awoke. He pulled the wheel with the boy, and together they watched the nightmare pass by the Glendora.

"Thank God for you, Emmanuel. We could be stove in on that hulk and perhaps be gone to a watery grave."

An old sailor's proverb says, "Keep your nose in the wind and your eye on the horizon." Emmanuel understood the message and became a worker to depend on. He mended ropes and did the chores decided by Mr. Mosher. Emmanuel was bone of his bone, flesh of his flesh.

To Mr. Mosher's great relief, Emmanuel never mentioned the floating derelict they'd seen that night. They say "sometimes the wound is in the soul, so it doesn't show openly." Mr. Mosher took inventory of his actions. The good fellow out of Lunenburg no longer carried the smell of rum on his breath.

The ship moved slowly north.

Off Cape Hatteras, the weather changed.

The crew battened down hatches, checked the ties on the cargo, and stowed the sails when the wind intensified. The wind in the rigging howled like banshees! Waves roiled.

Emmanuel happily went with the rest of his crewmates when all but the first mate were ordered below to wait out the gale.

Soon the first mate joined them too. He told them how the green seas flooded the deck. He assured the captain that the wheel was tied securely. "It is too wild to stay above."

Emmanuel learned why. "It is said that the eyes of fear are the largest."

Later, they would see the damage—a dory on deck smashed, barrels torn from the rails. Now they could only hold on and brace themselves as the Glendora dove into holes depressed into the sea and pitched upright again.

The crew gathered in the great cabin of the Glendora and pondered their fates.

"Many wreckers and salvage people have told of scams and shoddy fastenings in schooner construction to save a dishonest builder a few dollars..."

"Even though it could cost men's lives?"

"Even though."

That fear was in the minds of the crew.

Some were ready to pass judgment on Captain Knickle. They sized up their leader. They watched his steady hands. They watched his face and found no fear. They listened to his words, "The Glendora is properly built."

He pointed to a large framed picture on the cabin wall. The picture told the crew that Jesus walked on water.

"When you go through a trial, you need to believe in something greater than what happens."

Knickle's words and that image calmed the storm in their hearts.

The creaking and moaning sounds of the ship seemed to die away with the storm.

Once again, the crew believed as they rested from their labour on the third day. The Glendora would survive this as she had many other storms. The ship sailed on.

Emmanuel, the new citizen of the sea, also learned that real life must test a man, calling on his resources and love for others.

The rest of the voyage was uneventful.

When the Glendora passed Cross Island and entered Lunenburg Harbour, he saw a town of wooden houses built on hills.

This wasn't San Juan! He had never seen a town of all wooden buildings, and he had confusion when he compared what he saw to San Juan's concrete-like structures.

It was like a black-and-white photograph compared to the colour of Puerto Rico.

This harbour was full of ships like the Glendora. On the shore, he could see several ships being built and repaired at a shipyard with the steady noise of hammers and saws.

Men who had been working like the devil, paused to watch the Glendora as she blew in.

This two-masted vessel was decorated by sea for service done.

Once they were securely tied to the dock, Emmanuel became anxious. Where did he belong? He stayed on the ship while Captain Knickle made discreet inquiries to secure his prospects. Emmanuel was cold, despite the thick blanket he was wrapped in as he waited.

Eventually, the captain returned.

"Dr. Johnston and his good wife. They are childless. They have room for you."

Emmanuel soon discovered that Mrs. Johnson was also a very good and generous cook. And that this couple was to become his guardians.

In the big featherbed at Dr. Johnston's huge wooden house, Emmanuel lay awake in wonderment. This wasn't the dog-eat-dog world that sleeping rough in San Juan was. This big wooden house was almost castle-like and such space for just the doctor and his wife.

This boy was not yet fifteen. But he understood that, after his survival on the dangerous sea, he needed to believe in something greater than himself. A brush with death makes life matter. And he was determined to live a life that mattered.

Fishermen's Memorial, Lunenburg, Nova Scotia

THE NUNS' REFUGE
TOM ROBSON

If you visit the mid-Atlantic island of Madeira for longer than the eight-hour cruise ship stop, you may be enticed into visiting Curral das Freiras, the Nuns' Refuge. Most visitors take the modern road into the near vertical-sided bowl at the head of the thickly wooded valley where today's village nestles. Others look down on it, a thousand feet below, from Eira do Serado. From there, they may marvel that the narrow path down the near vertical-walled valley to The Refuge, was, until 1959, the only access.

More than four hundred years before the road from the coast was constructed, Filipa Ferreira wasn't marvelling at the view down into the valley. Its depths were obscured by the dense growth of trees and foliage clinging to its walls and covering the floor far below.

Filipa was dressed in the habit of a novitiate of the Order of Poor Clares. Her clothes were creased and far from clean, the hem was filthy and her footwear was as worn as her sandaled feet. A strand of black hair had escaped and, no matter how many times she tried to tuck it away, it drooped and hung across her sweat-and-dirt-stained face. But her engaging features showed an ethereal beauty in a young woman not enjoying this journey of her seventeenth summer.

The Abbess had ordered the sisters to rest before they started their perilous descent to their chosen place of safety. Already, they had walked more than twenty kilometres on the uneven and ever-uphill track from the Convent de Santa Clara, built on the fringes of the port of Funchal. It was a relief that the final part of their three-day journey was downhill, but Vincente, their guide, warned them of the dangers of the narrow, twisting path to their destination—their refuge.

The sighting of French pirate ships had prompted the emptying of their convent of its treasures and congregation. In her mind, Filipa cursed the latest of the rogues who wanted to plunder the rich island.

The convent and the church's valuables were transported by donkey. Those of the Poor Clares' congregation who were able had to walk. Some had been left behind. Many elderly nuns needed help, and the uphill pace had been very slow.

Pirates had raided Funchal, the largest settlement on Madeira, on many occasions. Vincente had told them that this time, a large, well-organized fleet intent on looting and killing was coming. Funchal was ill-prepared. The new fortress, Palacio de Sao Laurenco, was unfinished. The governor feared the indefensible town would be overrun. If so, the fate of the nuns at the hands of the heathen pirates couldn't be contemplated. This was why the sisters were fleeing to this remote hiding place inland, invisible and nearly impossible to find unless one was familiar with its location.

The first two days of the difficult, exhausting journey had prompted unkind thoughts in Filipa. They were directed at others, and she had so much to confess but wasn't sure when the next opportunity would arise. Father Horacio was with them. Perhaps there was a chapel at the bottom of this impossible chasm where she could make her confession.

Filipa thought enviously of her elder sister Esperanca, happily married and soon to set sail for Lisbon with her husband. Why couldn't Filipa have been the eldest and her sister the one forced to take the veil? Why had her parents given Filipa to God? The generous endowment could have provided a rich dowry for her. Did they really believe that they, as well as Filipa, would benefit spiritually from their gift of a daughter and money to the church?

Her father was a direct descendant of Adam Ferreira, the first Portuguese born on Madeira, but must these founding families follow custom? Must Filipa follow her ancestor into the order just because a daughter of the discoverer of the island became the convent's first abbess?

As Filipa sweated the climb in the summer heat of 1566, she had even questioned the existence of the convent, founded some seventy years before.

While they rested, Filipa tried to ignore these questions which were unworthy of one about to renounce her former life to devote herself to God. She offered prayers for the safety of her family, asking for her father and brothers to fight bravely to protect her sisters and mother. She also gave thanks for her escape from Funchal.

Stories of the fates of girls her age who fell into the clutches of pirates had been whispered before Filipa entered the convent. The previous day, she had shared these stories with Sister Madelene, who had recently made her final vows and who had been in the community from a very early age. Sister Madelene had been shocked to hear Filipa's gossip, and that evening under the stars, the two prayed while trying to sleep on the uncomfortable ground.

Three hours into today's climb, Vincente spotted the entrance to the descent to the refuge. Exhausted though many of the sisters were, Vincente had urged the abbess, Donna Irene, to start them down the pathway. This wasn't a descent to be made in threatening rain or after dark.

Filipa and Madelene were told to assist the elderly Sister Maria Gracea, who had refused to leave the convent. The abbess had insisted, promising help for her on the journey. Sister Maria Gracea's protests continued through this third day.

The surefooted donkeys were first led onto the steep and narrow path. Vincente followed. Donna Irene stayed at the back, with the normally severe and aloof Father Horacio offering help, encouragement, and prayers for the stragglers.

The footing was uneven, with rocks, roots, and loose dirt. There was always a sheer drop on one side of the ofttimes narrow path, with jutting rocks and whipping branches threatening to push the careless or unsteady traveller into the chasm. A fall would be fatal. Sister Maria Gracea tried to be careful, but she was so scared that she held tightly onto one or both of her younger sisters.

Progress, except by the surefooted donkeys, was slow. Rocks, stones, and dirt slipped from underfoot, rattling through the greenery into the depths. Filipa clung to roots and branches. She had given up trying to hold up her habit to avoid tripping over the hem, which was filthy and ripped after nearly three days in the mountains.

Again, Sister Maria Gracea stumbled. Again, both younger sisters pulled her to safety. On a broader shelf below, Vincente and the donkeys rested until others joined them. Once all the nuns were assembled and after belated noontime prayers, they shared a frugal meal of bread and water and olives. Donna Irene went among them, offering encouragement and assuring all that their next stop would be their destination. The nuns gave thanks for this welcome news.

Had the last stretch been uphill, some of them, including Sister Maria Gracea, wouldn't have reached the refuge. A further two-hour slow descent brought them to level ground below the near-vertical slope down which their path had zigzagged.

Peering between the trunks of huge trees, Filipa spotted some huts. Tethered outside were the donkeys. They had reached the refuge. Once there, all spontaneously knelt and gave thanks for deliverance from the dangers of that final descent.

Exhausted though they were, there was work to be done. The huts had been long abandoned and debris had to be cleared if the nuns were to sleep in them that night. Time and energy were lacking, but they undertook the tedious task of making the huts habitable. By nightfall, despite the bare earth floor and the holes in the walls and roof, the exhausted nuns slept, safe in their refuge.

Over the next few days, in their primitive quarters, the sisters tried to revert to the routines of their religious observances, which were centred on frequent prayers. Between these, under the guidance of Vincente, and with help from the few inquisitive locals who came to investigate their new neighbours, living quarters were improved, a chapel was established, and an outdoor kitchen and refectory created.

Filipa lost herself in the familiarity of re-established routines and the need to work on creature comforts for the community. At this time, the sisters relied on the energy and resilience of younger nuns.

She forgot doubts and questions that had come to the fore in the testing, physical challenge of the climb and the descent to Curral das Freiras. She neglected to share those doubts with Donna Irene, who perhaps would have had answers to her indecision and questions since Father Horacio wasn't yet taking confession.

But some days later, a commotion at the entrance to their clearing interrupted Filipa's work in the kitchen. Sisters fell to their knees, their prayers drowned out by sobs and crying. As Filipa investigated what had disturbed the peace of the new community, she noticed a young man speaking earnestly to Father Horacio. Though vaguely familiar, he was dishevelled, his features masked by dirt and sweat and, perhaps, blood. The clearly distressed youth could be Bartholome, a friend of her youngest brother, but he wasn't the upright, always smiling, handsome Bartholome she had known.

Above the sobbing noises issuing from the sisters, Donna Irene's raised voice implored her community to pray for the souls of the departed.

The kneeling Sister Maria Gracea glanced up from her prayers and saw the inquiring look on Filipa's face. She pulled Filipa to her knees. "Pray, Sister Filipa! Pray for the survival. Pray for the souls of your family. The French heathen ransacked the town and massacred those they captured at the new fort."

The young novice tried to compose herself, searching at her waist for her rosary, ashamed that she was thinking only of her loss and herself. "Are they all dead? Was my father there? And my brothers...?" Her futile questions tailed off.

"Bartholome is telling Father Horacio what he learned before he had to flee," Sister Maria Gracea said. "He says it's chaos in Funchal. Pray, Sister Filipa. Pray for God's mercy."

Filipa wanted to rush to the two men to discover the fate of her family. Sister Maria Gracea placed a restraining hand on her shoulder, and Filipa again bowed her head in prayer, following, with difficulty, her elder's example. She glanced up to see Father Horacio and Donna Irene escort Sister Madelene from the group. Filipa's tightly closed eyes couldn't diminish the cries of "No! No! Please, God. No!" that came from her friend.

Then came a tap on Filipa's shoulder. Father Horacio's usually gruff voice was gentle. "Sister, Donna Irene and I need to talk to you away from these prayers. Please come with me."

The priest helped Filipa to stand and took her elbow while they walked to the edge of the clearing where Donna Irene had isolated herself.

"No, Mother. No! Please. I beg of you!" The young novitiate spoke while fearfully approaching her superior. Donna Irene held the young woman while Father Horacio relayed Bartholome's news. Her father, her two brothers, and her sister's husband were among the prisoners slaughtered in the Palacio do Sao Lorenzo. Her older sister was safe with her mother, but she had lost the baby. The priest didn't explain how. He knew no more.

Filipa's knees buckled and a long, mournful wail came from deep within her. The priest and her abbess held her up, trying to comfort the bereft young woman.

After Filipa stopped crying, her questions began. But there were no details of events in Funchal. The only answer to "Why?" was one that Filipa's grief couldn't allow her to accept. "It is God's will, my child," gave no comfort and less satisfaction.

Sister Maria Gracea was summoned to her side as Donna Irene and Father Horacio gently raised and led another sister away from those kneeling in prayer. "What do I do, Sister Maria?" she asked in her grief. "I must go to them. I'm needed there!"

She was in shock. She needed to be sure of the truth of events in Funchal. She wanted another solution. Her distress led her to believe that to find either or both, she had to go to Funchal.

"The only answer is in prayer, my child." The older nun tried to comfort Filipa. "You have already left your family and are to renounce that life. You cannot change what God has ordained. You cannot help that family. You know that we are now your family. Accept us and accept God's holy will."

"But my mother and my sister—and what about the younger ones? Are they safe? I must go to them!"

Sister Maria Gracea was adamant. "No, little one. This is where you belong. You are their gift to the church."

Filipa was angered by this response. "And what did their gift bring in return from God? The Church will bury my father and brothers and I can't be there?" Then a solution came to her. "But I can. I can be with my mother and sisters. I must go. They need me now more than God does."

With that decisive, somewhat blasphemous outburst, Filipa broke from the consoling grasp of the older nun. She stood and looked around, seeing four other nuns reacting to news like that given to her. Stunned, all four seemed resigned to their suffering and accepting of consolation.

In contrast, Filipa resolved to act. She strode purposefully, to the start of the climb, out of the refuge, Curral das Freiras. She hitched up her habit at the waist to avoid tripping over it, and ignoring the shouted pleas from Father Horacio to return, she trudged up the path. Behind her, the pleas changed to angry orders to turn around and accept God's will.

Rapid footsteps approached Filipa from behind. She quickened her pace, a near impossibility on the severe upward slope.

"Wait, Filipa! It's me, Bartholome. I must return to Funchal. Will you let me escort you? We shall make the journey together."

Filipa let him catch up, hoping he was telling the truth and hadn't been sent to bring her back. If he was going to Funchal, he could explain more of what he had seen and heard. And a nun, traveling alone, even without getting lost, would be at risk. *Perhaps God will bless our journey,* she thought.

When Bartholome edged past, he reached behind to grasp her hand, pulling her up a particularly steep stretch. He voiced encouragement, "God willing, we can complete this climb before darkness falls." His voice provided the encouragement Filipa needed

"God willing!" Filipa replied.

Silently, she wondered whether God granted help to one who was fleeing from the refuge of the Church.

This story comes from a brief visit on such a vacation. It is based on a recorded, historical event and consequent journey to a now-famous location. The story composed and the characters described owe more to the writer's imagination than fact.

The Nuns' Refuge - Cural des Freiras - today as seen from Eira do Strada. This was, until the 1950s, the start of the only access , a steep and perilous pathway descending 1000 feet to the valley floor.

METAMORPHOSIS
JUDI RISSER

Cry out in confusion

Anguish over injustice

Rage at loss

Blood, fear and tears
Cascade down your worn and torn body
Broken, shrunken, humbled

The greater the force
The more intense, the shift

The deeper the gauge
The wider the rift

In being split wide open
We become completely whole

Suffering, shapes the soul.

INTO THE UNKNOWN
PHIL YEATS

He lurked in the shadows of the smoke-filled room, alone with his thoughts while nursing a beer. A serving girl doing her rounds said nary a word as she replenished his drink.

A blonde stole in and sat at the bar. The barman brought her something, placing it on the burnished mahogany counter. She stared at the glass without taking a sip and then stood and walked to the door.

The man from the shadows followed her out.

Outside the tavern, mayhem prevailed, with the mangled wreckage of one car T-boned into another dominating the late-afternoon scene. Police cars and emergency vehicles surrounded the pile of twisted metal, and uniformed figures scurried about.

The blond woman glanced at the scene, turned, and hurried away.

The man, now close behind, called out. "Please, don't run. I'm here to help." He took her arm and guided her across the street.

She pulled away as they approached a park. "Where are we?" she asked, eyes darting. "I was on my way home from work in a familiar neighbourhood, but here... I recognize nothing." Her hesitation suggested she struggled with unwelcome thoughts.

He sat on a bench by a pond teeming with ducks and patted the surface next to him. He waited, watching the birds milling around.

Tears welled in her eyes as she took a deep breath and acknowledged the truth. "I died in the accident, didn't I?"

"Yes, and that can't change. But I'm here to help you move forward to a future that's not as bleak as you fear. In fact, you should be pleased."

He watched as she processed his words. A young woman, perhaps twenty-five years old, five foot five or six, trim with no excess fat, but clearly a woman with subtle feminine curves. Her expression was sad, but she was quite beautiful with delicate features and shoulder-length ash-blond hair with just a hint of curl.

"So what are you?" she asked, finally accepting his offer and sitting on the bench. "An angel from Heaven or a demon from Hell?"

"Neither. I'm an emissary from a place of refuge for those who die too young."

"That sounds like Heaven, but will they admit me? I'm not religious. I mean I went to Mass every Sunday while growing up, but I stopped going."

"Don't worry, religion isn't important. We provide a home for people who die unexpectedly. One area is for elders who feel they died too soon. They can live in peace and serenity until they're comfortable with the idea no one lives forever. A second is for people who succumbed to incurable illnesses before their allotted threescore years and ten. They're given an opportunity to live out time taken from them. They're rewarded for their good deeds with a few years of extended life."

"So, it is like Heaven, rewarding people for doing good."

"But our definition of good is unlike that of most religions. Devotion to God doesn't count. Good Samaritans would be rewarded for their good deeds, not for their devotion. But I haven't mentioned our final area."

"Yes, tell me because I don't fit in the first two."

"We reserve the best places for innocent victims of crimes and natural disasters, events that take their lives, not just cause hardship. We try to make their sojourn in our world good and productive."

"If that's true, why not simply admit me at your version of the Pearly Gates and guide me down the path to the appropriate part of your magical kingdom?" She paused, apparently weighing something. "And what's your role? Are you conducting a test or some nasty initiation ceremony?"

"More like orientation. The transition is difficult and finding your place, not trivial. I'm here to guide you along the way and help you make the best choices."

"Wow! And I must accept whatever you decide?"

"No, the choices are always yours, and you can do it on your own if you prefer. I wouldn't recommend it because there's no on-line help to guide you. As I said, it is complicated, but it's your choice. And if you want a guide but don't want me, we'll find someone more to your liking."

She leaned back and stared at him, not trying to hide the fact she was making an appraisal. He wasn't concerned. His team began their assessment as soon as she died, and data came in fast and furious. They knew what sort of guy she dreamed about. Someone six feet tall, slim, well-toned but not muscle-bound, pleasant looking, neither a Hollywood-style hunk nor a ninety-eight-pound weakling. He fit the bill, and at twenty-nine, he was a good match for a twenty-six-year-old woman. Megan Fitzwilliam would accept him.

"You'll do," she said without enthusiasm. "And if I'm in charge, I'll call you Gary. So, that's decided, what's next?"

He was impressed. She had more gumption than he expected. "Gary it is, and the fact you didn't touch the drink we offered suggests you haven't eaten recently. Were you worried about the effect of strong liquor on an empty stomach?"

"Something like that. I was feeling lightheaded. It may have been lack of food or effects of the crash."

"Then dinner should be our next priority. Your choice. What do you prefer?"

"Anything I like?" He nodded, and she continued. "French. I've never been to an authentic French restaurant."

"That's what we shall have. And the only place for real French cuisine is Paris."

"What! We're going to Paris! You can't do that. It will be the middle of the night, and anyway, it takes hours to get there."

"No problem. We'll play fast and loose with time." He pointed to a spot on the path. "Now stand, right there in front of me."

A few seconds later, her skirt and T-shirt were transformed into an elegant royal-blue evening dress.

"What!" she exclaimed, looking down at herself. "Did you strip me naked here in a park? And this dress is too revealing!"

"Don't be silly. It only took a second; nothing could be seen. Watch." He stood in front of her as his clothes transformed into the formal eveningwear of a French gentleman in 1900. "Would you like to visit les Folies Bergère during la Belle Époque?"

"Oh, that would be so cool. We might even see Toulouse-Lautrec or another famous person."

"Come then. I offer you dinner at les Folies with Loïe Fuller doing her famous veil dance."

***

46

A flash of light and they were in 1890s Paris on the pavement outside the Folies Bergère. They swept in and found a small table near the stage. The food was more like a series of appetizers than the multi-course French meal he'd promised her, but exotic intoxicating drinks were plentiful, and he heard no complaints. Elaborate French cuisine would await another day.

The show started with dancers wearing diaphanous costumes and elaborate headdress prancing onto the stage.

"Oh, to be a dancer in that chorus," Megan exclaimed. "That would be so amazing!"

"If you want, I could arrange it."

She held her hands in front of her mouth and stared wide-eyed. She said nothing but nodded her head. An instant later, she appeared in costume amongst the dancers.

At the end of Loïe Fuller's provocative veil dance, Megan reappeared at their table, once again wearing her blue dress. "How did you manage that? How did I know what to do? And did you notice Miss Fuller? She was stark naked at the end!"

He smiled. No one would have missed Loïe Fuller's nudity, but he focused on Megan's reaction to her own performance. Their research described her as a shy person with no boyfriend and little social life. Her participation in any public performance, much less one where she was almost as naked as Ms. Fuller at the culmination of her dance, was unexpected.

They remained in the club for several hours. Toulouse-Lautrec appeared as the show ended and presented Megan with a drawing of a chorus girl.

"It's me," she exclaimed. "And I look, well... almost naked." She sighed. "It was so much fun, and I don't care how exposed I was. If my library colleagues saw me, they would be *so* jealous."

Gary stood, passed the artist several bank notes, and offered Megan his hand. "Should we be going?"

"I guess we must. But where? Where are we going?"

"A hotel, of course. I reserved a suite in a fine hotel, and tomorrow we shall enjoy the sights of Paris: the Louvre, the newly opened Eiffel Tower, anything you desire. But I have one request. May we return to the twenty-first century? Reproducing the world of 1890 is difficult."

She looked at the old-fashioned street scene with horse-drawn carriages. "It has been amazing, but if it's too difficult..."

"Then tonight, when we retire, it will be 1890, but in the morning, 2015."

"What's all that?" she asked as a liveried bellman pulled a cart piled high with suitcases through the majestic front doors of their hotel.

"Why your luggage," Gary replied as he passed her a handful of documents. "These are your papers. You are Miss Fitzwilliam of Halifax, Canada, recently arrived from New York on the Cunard Liner *Etruria*."

Registration completed, they entered their suite.

"Wow!" Megan exclaimed after the bellman deposited their bags in the sitting room, took the tip Gary offered him, and departed. "This is so fancy! I mean, does Buckingham Palace have furnishings like this?"

Gary laughed. "I suspect Queen Victoria would consider this rather plain."

Megan skipped to a little vestibule. "They said there were two bedrooms. A small one for my secretary. That's you. You're listed on the paperwork as a family retainer? Did you notice the clerk's face when he read that?"

Gary nodded.

"Bathroom," she said after opening the first door and moving to the second. "And this must be your room. No, it's too big. Can this be the main bedroom?"

"No, that's the smaller one."

"Oh, my God," Megan exclaimed as she disappeared into the third room. "It's huge. There's another bathroom and a tiny maid's room." She poked her head back into the sitting room. "They offered me a maid for the duration of our stay, but I declined. Were they thinking of her as a chaperone? And we're registered for three nights. You know that, don't you?"

"Yes. That gives us two days to tour Paris."

Megan crossed the sitting room and sat next to Gary. He held up a glass with amber liquid. "Would you like one?"

"No. I've had more than enough to drink. Tell me what's going on. I was killed in a car crash, and you arrived to escort me to a mysterious after-world. So, what are we doing in 1890s Paris in an opulent hotel for three nights?"

"We needed a place for dinner, and you chose French cooking."

"Don't give me that. Halifax has French restaurants. We needn't travel through time and space to Paris in 1890. And anyway, we didn't get the multi-course French dinner I requested."

"We still have two nights. I promise you two elaborate multi-course Parisian dinners. And the show, you must agree, was worthwhile."

"Yes, les Folies were wonderful. And an original drawing by Henri de Toulouse-Lautrec. That was beyond wonderful."

"And your participation in Loïe Fuller's veil dance?"

"Another incomparable experience. But you're avoiding my question."

"You sure you wouldn't like a drink?" She shook her head, and he poured himself another. "The transition to our world is difficult. Newcomers need time for reflection during these transitional days. A few wonderful new experiences also help."

"Fine. I have my amazing experiences. Shouldn't we get over there?"

"Not so fast. There's time, a week or ten days, for other experiences, but mostly you need to consider two things. First, you must deal with the things you will never do because you died unexpectedly. They may be simple things we can accomplish over the next days, or more complex ones that can't be solved in a week, or maybe ever."

"More experiences here on Earth? Rome would be nice, but what I will miss is falling madly in love with someone and having a baby. Can you do anything about those?"

"A baby won't be possible, but nothing should stop you from falling in love."

She looked at the open door to the larger bedroom. "So, no baby, but I can anticipate romantic relationships. With you perhaps?"

"Possible, but let's not jump too quickly because we have another task. You must identify what you would like to accomplish during your forty-four years in your new home."

"Forty-four years?"

"Yes, to make up what remains of your threescore years and ten. You need to make them productive."

"But that's what I've been saying. Wouldn't it be better to see how it works and how I can fit in before I decide?"

"We've determined this is the best way to proceed."

She shrugged her shoulders. "I will try to be patient, but—"

He held up his hand. "Don't say it. I should describe our world." She nodded, and he continued. "First, it's a beautiful, uncrowded place, an easy place to live. Food, clothing, and shelter are readily available, so there's no struggle for survival. You can simply conjure up anything you need."

"Are you trying to tell me we're already in this mysterious new place, in a computer-game-like virtual reality you've conjured up? The bar I visited after the crash, the park where you started explaining things, and all these images of Paris, were they real?"

"They're real enough, and you will soon produce similar images, but you must learn to develop positive images, not negative self-destructive ones, and conjure up useful things that help you move forward."

"Move forward to what? I mean, I'm dead, what's there to move forward to?"

"An opportunity to accomplish something with the time we're returning to you. You can write a great novel, create wonderful pieces of art, research important scientific concepts, or endless other possibilities. Or you can provide for others, babies, for example. When babies die here on Earth, they arrive in our world alone and helpless. We must care for them, help them grow and develop."

"Or I could be like you and help newcomers make the transition."

"Yes, that's another way to be a provider."

"What if I suggested transitioning was something I wanted to do?"

"We would discuss it while we tour Paris, or drive through the French wine country, or bask on a beach in the Riviera."

"But what's to discuss? It's either something I would like to do, or it's not."

He shook his head. "Nothing is ever that simple. Think about it. I spend a month helping someone like you transition, then I'm home for a week before I'm off again. Not the easiest life if I'm interested in a relationship with someone else. And maintaining a relationship would be impossible for two transitioners."

"If I chose that role, I'd limit my opportunities for a relationship, and one with you'd be off the table. Is that why you said we should put off any decisions about, you know, getting together in my marvellous canopy bed?"

"Yes, and you should consider other choices, like working in the crèche system for infants. Then you could experience all aspects of raising a child except having one. It might be a good choice."

"And I might still find true love and... other pleasures?"

"So much to consider, but not tonight. It's late and we should retire, for one night at least, to our separate beds."

***

A week later, they were on the Côte d'Azur, at a secluded beach in an area of upscale homes. They'd been to Cannes and several other areas frequented by the hoi polloi but settled on this exclusive neighbourhood of the rich and famous.

"I've thought about my choices," Megan said as they sat on the beach engaging in one of her favourite activities, trying to identify famous people among the passers-by.

"And what have you decided?"

"One serious possibility was your job of transitioner. It's interesting because it's both helpful to others and allows me to maintain contact with my old world. I agree it's not ideal for an intimate relationship, but not impossible except for one with another transitioner."

"So you and I couldn't develop a relationship."

"Would that disappoint you?" When he nodded but said nothing, she continued. "This has been my most intense relationship ever, and letting it go would be difficult. That gets me to my second possibility."

"Carry on."

She took a deep breath. "Working in a crèche and planning to be the prime caregiver for one or more babies."

"The whole surrogate mother thing?"

"Yes, as much as possible."

"And that choice would give you a better chance of developing an intimate relationship with another adult."

"Yeah, including an ongoing relationship with one sexy transitioner," she said, wriggling closer. "But I'd change his name from Gary to something else."

"Why, what's wrong with Gary? You chose it."

"Gary is a name destined for the trash heap. I wouldn't want a long-term companion whose name was headed for the dumpster."

"I'm not supposed to influence you, but I like the sound of that choice."

"Are you joking? You've been influencing me this whole week. Or do you behave in the same romantic way with all your 'clients'?"

He tried to pull away from her increasingly obvious embrace. "I had sex with some 'clients' as you call them, but never anything as serious as this."

Megan clapped her hands. "Good, I hoped I was getting more than the standard transition package. Now, we must consider option three."

"We still have several days. Why don't we move on to Italy, the Leaning Tower of Pisa, or Rome with the Coliseum and Sistine Chapel?"

"Yeah, let's hop in that monstrous red Ferrari and seek another adventure."

"But before we go, what is idea number three?"

"Well, you know I worked at one time in the university's theology school library."

Gary nodded. If their research was as good as it was cracked up to be, he should have expected idea number three to involve religion. "Yes. It doesn't match well with your lack of allegiance to a church."

"I haven't gone to church for years, but I was raised in the Catholic Church, and I read and thought about theology. If your people aren't immortal, there's still a role for theological discourse. I can imagine it as a stepping stone between Earth, and Heaven or Hell and contemplate its significance."

"This sounds serious. Not something to discuss as we rocket down the highway at one hundred and fifty kilometres per hour."

"People like the street racer who killed me would go straight to Hell, the Dante's Inferno kind of hell, without interaction with your world. Others who've had a full life would proceed to the place of judgement or whatever it is one normally faces when they die."

"Assuming life after death exists."

She spread her arms wide and looked around. "But it must. Otherwise, how do you explain this little adventure we're on? It's an intermediate life for those whose time was cut short, a place where they can strive to be useful. When they die, they will join the others at the gates of Heaven, and because your world encourages accomplishments and good deeds, their chances would be improved. Otherwise, none of this makes sense."

"That's an interesting concept, so a good option. But there are issues to ponder as we tour the home of Roman Catholicism."

"Like what?"

"Our world has no churches, temples, or mosques. There's no adversity, no danger, no struggles to make ends meet, so we have little need for religion. How will an essentially religion-free world fit the picture you're developing?"

"So, no opportunity to be pious. You'd have to impress the guardians of the Pearly Gates by being useful, not by being devoted."

"Wouldn't that be an issue? Puts the kibosh to those who wallow in the trappings of religion."

"But that would be an improvement! Actually having to do something good, rather than just look like you're a good person, would be beneficial."

"I can see you're really into this. Let's pack our stuff and hit the road. This evening we can sit in a café guzzling Italian wine and pontificate. Get it Pontif-icate, appropriate, don't you think?"

"That's the stupidest pun I've heard in months. But let's do it. Visit Italy before moving on to your Shangri-La. When I arrive, I can combine working in a crèche, contemplating these theological questions, and making out with a handsome transitioner who makes terrible puns. My new world will be a blast, and maybe I can improve my chances of getting into Heaven!"

This story is intended as a light-hearted look at life after death and religion. Obviously, none of it can have any basis in real life.

JOURNEY TO FREEDOM
MAIDA FOLLINI

Friends Church (Quakers) in Maple Grove, Maine, near the border with New Brunswick at Perth Andover, was a station on the Underground Railroad during the 1850s and '60s. The Quakers of the Friends Church helped conduct escaping African Americans, hiding them in the church cellar, or in a space underneath the preacher's platform, or in the bell tower. From the church, the escaping people were helped into a small boat on Monson Pond and rowed across the pond to the New Brunswick border. There they were met by helpers and taken in by black communities along the St. John River. This story is a fictionalized account of what a family would have gone through to reach freedom in Canada.

It had been a long, cold ride from Quaker Whiting's place. My little sister and I had turned out of the haymow before it got light, drank hot mugs of cocoa in Mrs. Whiting's kitchen, and then back to the barn where Ma talked with Mr. Whiting about how to hide us in his farm cart.

"Dawn's coming, pretty quick," old Whiting said. "Got to get you out of sight before the hired men come over to care for the stock."

Ma rescued the blanket we had all slept in, shook the hayseed off it, and wrapping it around Naomi, lifted her into the wagon. Mr. Whiting raised the cover of the wagon seat where he would sit to drive. I scrambled into the box, followed by Naomi who needed a little help because she was only five. My legs were longer, as I have had two more years to grow. I could stretch out full length, but Ma had to curl up to fit herself in.

"Here, Naomi, you lie on top of me," she said to my sister, "and Ruth, you squidge down beside me." Squidge down it was. I had to lie on my side to fit, but I didn't care. I felt safe when Ma was with us. We shared our warmth, pressed altogether with the blanket on top of us, covering us over, in case anyone lifted the wagon seat's top. When Mr. Whiting took his seat above us, the wood creaked with his weight. Good that he was heavy, I thought. So long as he was sitting there, no one could open the top.

It grew colder, the farther north we went. We bumped through what Mr. Whiting said was northern Maine, with the horses clopping, the wagon rattling, and the wheels grinding. Folded up in the wagon box, we lay still, in a state of hibernation like the bears in winter—shutting down, not moving—just getting through the cold time.

I think Ma was scareder than me; I could feel her tense whenever the wagon stopped, and men's loud voices were heard talking to Mr. Whiting. I knew better than to ask Ma questions—she had told us to act as if we had no tongues, not to cough or sneeze even, muffle up any noise, and we better not make even our stomachs rumble lest the bounty hunters hear us and take us back to the plantation.

The plantation meant home—with Aunt Sarah, Uncle Meshak, the familiar smells of the cooking fires, the pigs we had to feed. But since Pa had left, it wasn't the same. I hadn't known he would leave. He talked late at night, after we were in our bunk, but Ma never told us what he said. Just one morning, he was gone. And then Sneeden, the overseer, came round and made trouble for Ma, and didn't believe her when she said she didn't know nothing, and said he would sell us—sell Naomi and me!—to a man down the road who was looking for likely girls! That's when Ma got tense and quiet. She stopped smiling and went quietly at night to talk to who knows who? And came back to the cabin, not saying where she'd been.

A few days later, Ma woke us up in the middle of the night and told us not to make a sound. She wrapped blankets around us, and we stole out of the cabin—no moon that night. She led us by her hand down to the stream, and she made us walk *in* the stream! Which usually she yells at us for getting wet! And we walked way behind the neighbours' farm, then left the stream and went through a grove of woods, to a rutty back road and there was old Tophet waiting with his buggy, an old black man who used to go around delivering moonshine to the back doors of houses—and he took us up, and put a tarpaulin over us, and drove us off. That was the beginning of our journey.

When there was a chance to talk at a safety house, Ma told us we would join Pa in Canada way up north, but we had to keep still as a mouse—stiller than that—still as a stone. I think Naomi had forgotten how to talk as she hadn't hardly made a sound on this trip. And me, I was just bursting to talk, but I held it in and swallowed it, till it made a lump in my stomach.

Anyway, we got to Whitings' farm, which they said was in Maine, and we could sit around the farm kitchen table while Mrs. Whiting cooked us the best meal I'd eaten in a long time—roast pork and white potatoes mashed up with brown gravy dripping all over them. And an apple pie for dessert. I felt like staying right there, but Ma said it wasn't safe. And the Whitings made sure the curtains were drawn on the windows so no one would see us, even though the house was way out on a country road, with no neighbours around.

The next morning, we climbed into the wagon box and went on up the road toward the north—towards Canada, wherever that was. It was a long, cramped day. Sometimes I dozed beside Ma, sometimes I was restless and kept wriggling around, trying to shift my sore bones. Ma would hiss at me, and I would stay still awhile. I knew she felt sorer than I did, with her knees almost up to her chin and Naomi asleep on her chest.

But finally, we got to this place—Friends Church, it was called, and we could hardly climb out of the wagon box, we were so stiff. The people at the church took us inside and tried to warm us up near a small woodstove. They were having a Quaker Meeting, and while they prayed and sang, others gave us bread and milk, and Ma had coffee. One woman brought over a cake with icing on it and gave it to us girls—Ma had some, too. They showed us where we had to sleep that night because the church had to look empty after the service was over and everyone went home. The stove had to be damped down, the lanterns had to be put out, and we had to be out of sight in case someone thought there was anyone in the church at the wrong time.

They took us down some stairs that led into the earth, I thought, but it was the basement, dark, damp and smelly. There were two rooms— one hidden behind the other, behind a door that looked just like a wall with shelves on it, to hide that it was a door.

The men brought in some horse blankets. We put one on the earth floor and lay down under the other one. I was so tired I didn't care about the dark and the smells. I just went right to sleep.

"Tomorrow, we'll be in Canada," Ma said. And sure enough, next day, they took us through the woods, to a pond, where we got in a boat, and the boat had to knock through chunks of ice and steer down a long dark lake. Ma crouched down with Naomi and me, sitting in the bottom of the boat. A man—I never knew his name, he didn't say—put a horse blanket over us all to hide us in case anyone walked along the shore, even though it was wild country and there were no houses around. We could hear the creaking of the oars in the oarlocks and the splash of water. After a long while, the boat bumped against the shore. Some men lifted us out and said, "You're in Canada now."

I looked around. It didn't look any different—just snow in the cold woods and ice on the lake.

The new people—the Canadians—didn't seem afraid. They were smiling and cheerful, and talked loudly, "Come on, not far now. We have a wagon to take you to town." We didn't have to hide in the wagon—we sat up on the seats like regular people. The men asked questions. Ma answered guardedly—she was still tense.

But when we got to the town, there was a bunch of folks, white and black, waiting at a community hall, and there, there was Pa! So tall, his head above the crowd!

"Oh, my God. Thank you!" said Ma, and she clung to him. Naomi and I, we grabbed his legs and hung on, never wanting to let go.

Friends Church, Maple Grove, Maine, winter, 2014. Here local Friends concealed African-American men, women, and children who had escaped from slavery in the American South. The next step was to row them across a lake to Canada on the other shore.

ADVENTURES ALONG THE WAY

A WOODSMAN'S NEAR-DEATH EXPERIENCE (A LESSON IN HUMILITY)
JOHN GABRIEL

A forest can be unimaginably enchanting but also unpredictable. Jumping in on top of a bear's meal while he is busy eating is just one of those unpredictabilities—dangerous, to be sure, but just another day in the life of a Canadian woodsman. For some years, as a lumberjack, I had been working in the forests of western Canada. I was a seasoned woodsman and looked forward to each day's work. Of other jobs I tired, but the woodlands were a special place to me and a place I felt at home. But a forest teeming with wild life has more than its fair share of surprises—some nice and some not.

Across the forest hillside, the late morning sun set its warmth as I made my way in search of salvageable fallen cedar trees, wood to be manufactured into shakes and shingles to adorn the roofs of houses. Ahead, however, a massive tree lay horizontally across my path, compelling me to climb over it. Driving my axe into its upper crust, I pulled myself to the top and dropped to the far side.

It could be said that looking before one leapt was a wise precaution, but that was not what I had done. I should have.

I inadvertently dropped in on a bear's meal—the half-eaten remains of a deer, and beside the remains, the one that was feasting on it—a black bear. My situation was dire.

Fear ripped through me as a scythe cuts through grass. My world came to a standstill—my body froze in fear. However, even in the strangling clutch of terror, from deep within the call to stay alive surged.

But what to do in that moment, I didn't know. The bear, too, was taken by surprise and retreated—but by the slightest margin. He then turned and prepared to attack.

I was truly alone and confronted with death—a gruesome one at that. The thought of being ripped apart by the steel-like claws of the forest dweller and stashed away in the ground for his next meal was unsettling.

Through the fog of fright, my inner voice urged me not to run but to use the only weapon I had and confront the animal—my woodsman's axe. An axe was something I used skillfully. I had for years used it in the splitting and hewing of wood, but never before had I used it as a weapon. I would live or die within the following seconds.

The fear that had paralyzed me eased as I prepared to charge, my focus locked on the rusty spot that marked the bear's brow—there I would make a strike. There was no room for compassionate thinking if I wanted to stay alive.

My war-like Celtic screech echoed on and on across the valley as I made my charge. Unfortunately, I didn't get far. My foot caught a bump, tossing me toward the claws of my nemesis, my screaming and yelling blunted by the generous helping of dirt that pushed itself into my mouth as I hit the ground face first. Then, the bear was upon me. His claws raked through my flesh as his scissor-like teeth ripped out my body, chunk by chunk.

It was all so real, so terrifying; it was what I expected, but that didn't happen.

Suddenly, the woodlands grew quiet. Moments later, it burst alive with nature's calls: the wind through the trees, birds chirping, the stream's flow, butterflies fluttering, and squirrels chirping. I was alive—the bear had fled. Nonetheless, my heart pounded its frantic beat, a beat laced with relief but encrusted in the aftershocks of a very bad near-death experience.

Was the bear to return? I didn't know. I prayed it wouldn't. Exhausted and afraid, I left the scene; unfortunately, not by way of my arrival. Out of confusion and shock, I chose a different path.

In my fear-borne retreat, I chanced upon a steep, fast-flowing mountain creek.

I had little choice but to attempt a crossing. I was fortunate. Across the thundering waters lay a long, narrow cedar tree. Steadying on its sturdy trunk, I warily moved toward the far bank.

A hint of life returned to my traumatized form as the cool of the mountain stream splashed upon my bloodied face—my pain-raked body. But as predictable as trees grow in a forest and night follows day, my moments of recovery were to be challenged. From the opposite side of the creek, a creature of peculiar appearance ambled toward me.

Taken aback, I raised my voice, hoping to make him backtrack, to no avail. As he continued toward me, once again fear seized me as my eyes set upon a body clad in spiked armour.

The forest traveler was a porcupine, a creature not even a grizzly bear would tangle with. My situation proved perilous. The tree—narrow, wet, moss-covered, and slippery—made any retreat impossible; however, I brandished a mighty fine weapon—my axe.

Across the forest's shadows, the sun's blinding glare reflected the weapon's razor-edged steel. I'd had enough of forest dwellers—with good reason—and this one surely would die.

Not more than a metre from me, the bundle of quills waddled toward its death. However, I had to be cautious to the extreme. One miscalculation would send me tumbling into the thundering, ice-cold waters.

Stabbing my spiked logging boots firmly into the beam, I braced myself for the inevitable one-sided battle.

As I raised the lethal weapon, a great interference from my nicer side jabbed at me. My heart wouldn't allow the killing. It was with much reluctance that I eased down from the crossover into the brutal rush of the frigid stream, thereby allowing the lowly creature safe passage while the ice-cold waters added only to my pathetic miseries and dragged me across its slithery moss-covered boulders.

Eventually, bruised, bleeding, and grazed, I reached the safety of the bank. Looking back toward the critter that had caused me such misery, I watched as he entered the forest undergrowth. Without affording me a simple glance—an appreciation of my kindness toward him—he disappeared from my life forever and left behind on the banks of the stream, something of no importance—me. To be sure, I got the full comprehension of what humility was all about.

Seventy-One Miles of Mud and Sweat
Janet McGinity

Two men stopped at the pool's edge, faces red with exertion after dragging the kayak a quarter mile along the grassy slope, all that was left of the Portobello Inclined Plane in Dartmouth. Dead leaves and pondweed floated gently in the pool.

"I'll put her in here," said Peter, shoving the kayak over the edge. Holding the bow of the boat, he stepped off the bank. A slop of water and thick black ooze bubbled over the tops of his sneakers, up his legs to his thighs. He staggered and tried to regain his balance.

"Holy crap, it's a lot deeper than it looks."

On the towpath, his buddy Dave Pyke watched, aghast. A big, burly man, he could have slipped to his death, or at least sunk in much deeper, if he had tried to put in the boat instead of the lighter Peter. Both wore lifejackets, but as non-swimmers, there wasn't much either could do. The distance between the water surface and the ooze was only a few inches, too little to float the kayak with two men in it.

Dave walked along the bank a few yards until the water deepened and then climbed into the seat behind Peter. Relieved at their escape, they paddled to the end of the pool and exited at the path that led to the next lake in their route. A minute or two later, they were in the open water of Lake William.

A few months earlier, Peter had purchased a copy of *Canoe Routes of Nova Scotia*. An avid paddler, he was often joined by his buddy Dave in his explorations. His boat was a hybrid canoe/kayak called a Mallard, open on top like a canoe but propelled with kayak paddles. It was very stable and hard to tip.

One route caught his eye. It was the Shubenacadie Canal System, a chain of streams, lakes, and the Shubenacadie River running seventy-one miles from Dartmouth on Halifax Harbour to Maitland at the Bay of Fundy. It followed an old Mi'kmaq route, traversing the Nova Scotia mainland.

The canal opened in 1861 after decades of stop-and-start building. It saw ten short years of boat traffic before it was superseded by the new Intercolonial Railway in 1870 and closed for good. Nowadays, the canal attracted only recreational watercraft.

Dave was immediately interested in the idea of paddling the canal system.

"How about we do the whole thing in a weekend?" Dave suggested, but Peter thought that might be too much, especially if they ran into problems.

"Here's an alternative," said Peter. "We could do it in stages, over a couple of summers. That seems more workable."

They checked out distances and the all-important high tide times and ranges along the Shubenacadie River component. The river was tidal for about twenty miles from Maitland inland to Milford Station. The canoe routes map indicated that parts of it were dangerous for small craft, especially where a series of huge waves called a tidal bore roared upstream from the Bay of Fundy.

Dave and Peter spent several weekends driving the planned route, choosing where they would put in, preferably below a bridge with an area to park a vehicle. Dave's wife Cynthia and daughter Roxanne would meet the paddlers with a second vehicle at the end of each stage.

On a summer day in 1998, the two men carried the Mallard to the water's edge at Lake Banook in Dartmouth. Cynthia and Roxanne cheered as the men waded into the lake. They paddled the calm waters of Lake Banook into Lake Micmac, and then through the Deep Cut, a mile-long passage cut through bedrock, into Lake Charles.

"Look, you can still see where they blasted." Peter pointed to the mossy stone blocks lining the narrow passage. "Must have been a huge job. It apparently took two entire construction seasons just to build this section."

They followed the map, taking a breather after the near-emergency at the Portobello Inclined Plane. Nearly a century and a half earlier, a marine railway hauled canal boats along this slope to the next waterway, where they were dropped to continue their journey. Some carried mining equipment for the gold mines at Montague and Waverley.

Peter and Dave passed through Lake William and Lake Thomas, whose shores were lined with homes and cottages, and into Lake Fletcher. Shortly after paddling beneath a bridge under Highway 102, Dave spied Inn on the Lake and two figures waving at them from the lawn. It was Cynthia and Roxanne. The four had lunch at the Inn to celebrate accomplishing the first stage of their journey.

Later that summer, they accomplished the second stage. This time, they paddled in the opposite direction, from Oakfield Provincial Park on Shubenacadie Grand Lake to Inn on the Lake, a convenient stop for a meal and rendezvous with Cynthia.

To this point, they had travelled through smaller lakes. Grand Lake was a different story. It had a reputation for fierce winds and squalls. Luckily, the weather was kind. They started on the lake early in the morning before the winds strengthened and had no trouble making the passage. Along the way, frolicking otters watched them pass.

Stage Three took another day of paddling, in August of 1998, from Oakfield Provincial Park to Milford Station, where the Shubenacadie River became tidal. But having left this stretch of the journey late, there was much less water in the river, and they found themselves dragging the kayak almost as much as they paddled it.

Stage Four occurred on a summer day in 1999. Dave and Peter put the kayak in at Milford Station, planning to paddle downstream and then leave the river and travel a short distance up Rynes Creek, a small tributary. A bridge crossed the Shubenacadie River at this point. Beneath it was a small parking area, where Cynthia would meet them.

Along the way, the river changed from a clear stream to a ruddy chocolate, lined with glistening clay banks, salt marshes, and rich pastures. It meandered in a series of oxbows, almost folding back on itself. Bald eagles soared above, watching for an easy meal of floating dead fish. Mink darted out from behind grass tufts on the shore. Fishermen waved from the banks as they passed.

The powerful tide carried the kayak downstream at a tremendous clip, and soon, Peter and Dave saw the bridge over Rynes Creek and turned the boat into the inlet to paddle towards the parking spot. It was indeed "low water"—only about a foot of it—not enough to float a boat carrying two men up the creek.

"Oh, damn! I must have miscalculated," moaned Peter. "I thought it would be hours before the tide dropped this much." He thought quickly. "Dave, you get out and walk beside the boat. That will lighten it, and it will float a little higher. I'll paddle."

Dave heaved himself out of the kayak. The bottom of the creek was a jelly-like mass of water and clay mud that rose over his boots and cleaved to his legs.

"I'm going to friggin' sink up to my eyebrows!"

Panicked, Dave grabbed the gunwale, which made the boat tip towards him. Peter leaned hard in the other direction, and Dave let go. When the boat wobbled sideways, Peter flailed and slid out of the boat onto the creek bottom. They groaned and looked up at the eight-foot distance to the top of the bank.

"Only thing to do—we'll both have to pull the boat up the bank."

Peter got out and the two started to drag the kayak up the slippery bank. It was a Sisyphean climb, with the sticky clay sucking at their legs. By the time they collapsed, exhausted, on the grass, they were covered in mud from ankles to armpits.

"Only one more stage to go—thank God," Peter breathed.

The map indicated that the last stretch of the river to Maitland was "highly tidal" and shouldn't be attempted except by "very competent white-water paddlers." The two friends decided to check out how dangerous it was—or maybe wasn't. They booked a Tidal Bore Rafting expedition.

Several companies operated these adventure tours from Maitland and other nearby sites. The tidal bore charging upstream overpowered the river's downstream current and generated whirlpools and turbulence. Rafting tours were most exciting during a full or new moon when tides were at their highest. Zodiac inflatable rafts churned through the six- to eight-foot waves, spraying water over passengers hanging onto alarmingly fragile-looking polypropylene ropes. It felt like riding a rollercoaster.

Peter and Dave chose a four-hour tour. As the pack of rubber rafts jostled around the wildest part of the tidal bore, one of the other boats flipped, and a woman landed in the churning river. She was hauled aboard by another boat.

"Sweet Jesus," Dave said, recalling the incident later. "She had a look of horror in her face, and then I saw her buttocks flop open so that I could see her pelvic bone—she was nearly cut in two by the outboard motor.

"They called an ambulance, and it picked her up where a bridge crossed over the river," he added. He learned later that the woman had survived the mishap.

Dave and Peter agreed that this section seemed do-able in the Mallard as long as they didn't attempt it when the tidal bore came in. They decided to paddle on a dropping tide, which would carry them along with little effort on their own behalf.

Stage Five was accomplished later that summer. The two men put the Mallard in at Rynes Creek and paddled out to the Shubenacadie

River. The tide was on the ebb, but the river was still deep. So far, so good. But by the time they arrived near Maitland, the Mallard grounded on a large sandbar in the middle of the river. They dragged the boat across it to a channel nearer the shore, where they could continue to paddle towards the mouth of the river. Finally, the docks and houses of Maitland appeared on the shore: the end of the journey.

A celebratory barbecue and a few beers were set for a summer's evening. The voyage was the most challenging either man had ever done. They felt quietly proud of their accomplishment, a journey comprised of "seventy-one miles of mud and sweat."

Peter Richard remembers the next stage of his journey on the Shubenacadie Canal System, at the Portobello Inclined Plane.

WIND AND WEATHER PERMITTING
WILMA STEWART-WHITE

Summer at the cottage. The phrase summons a kaleidoscope of snapshots that gladden my heart. Early morning tea on the beach steps, watching the resident grumpy great blue heron doing his invisible routine while fishing. The lone canoeist edging the cove in a rising mist. A doe leading her fawn across a narrow isthmus for breakfast on the little island. The blue-and-white sailboat tugging gently at the mooring, hopeful for a day's sail. Memories of big and small grandchildren tumbling on the lawn and swinging in the hammock.

Some days are clearer than others. This day remains very clear...

The sun was a golden ball behind my eyelids. In bliss, I lay supine on my sun lounger. I faintly heard ice cubes sliding and melting in my iced tea. The knowledge that my new murder mystery was an arm's reach away completed my satisfaction.

Suddenly, a shadow blocked my view. Rick, my husband, leaned over me, interrupting my idyllic moment. "Beautiful day for our sail, dear," he reminded me.

On that hot and sunny Saturday in July, the view from the cottage deck was picture perfect. The only flaw was the blue-and-white sailboat bobbing at its mooring—a siren call for Rick.

So far that summer, I had avoided the dreaded "overnight sail," but that weekend, I hadn't sidestepped fast enough.

I sighed and went into the kitchen. A stack of food storage boxes, a basket of wine, and a cooler awaited me on the kitchen table. We gathered them and began the journey: down the steps to the beach, into the cockleshell dinghy, rowed the dinghy out to the boat, up the ladder to the cockpit, down the steps into the galley.

In case of inclement weather or gusty wind, everything had to be well-secured, so we stowed everything safely away. We raised the jib, hoisted the mainsail, made sure the dingy was safely attached. Then we let go of the mooring and were off to sea, and I watched my comfortable spot on the deck recede.

I eyed the white full-bellied sail and admired the vessel slicing through the waves.

We charted a course out and around our own little Crow Island and headed for the tiny Nubble, one of many small islands scattered in the bay. We skimmed by Oak Island wrapped in its secrets. Was there really a treasure buried deep in a shaft? I imagined a swarthy captain with an eye patch and cutlass watching his sweaty crew dig deeper and deeper while chests of gold and silver were piled beside the hole. The trusty first mate in his striped jersey held the map with important clues. Had this ever happened? Or was it nonsense, wishful thinking, or legend? Certainly, a large audience watched weekly to follow the televised hunt of today's search.

The intense bowl of the sky was only broken by huge cumulous clouds scudding by. The deep blue ocean had small puffy waves, all picture perfect until we rounded the point where the wind seemed much stronger. The mainsail protested as we hauled it in. The jib quivered and then bellied out. The waves got choppier, and suddenly a strong gust heeled us over, dipping the rail.

We scrambled to the high side, bracing ourselves.

The bow left trails of silvery ruffles as we built up and got underway. The speed increased, and we bowled along. Our mild afternoon sail was building.

I had difficulty finding secure footing. Rick suggested I go forward on the bow, which I did with great caution as the boat was still well-heeled over.

The only safe place turned out to be spread-eagled on the deck, with fingers and toes holding onto cleats. Just as I positioned myself, lightning cracked, and the heavens opened. Huge raindrops pummelled us.

The ocean raced by. Waves from the bow crashed over me. I was immersed in cold, salty water and miserable, but no rescue seemed at hand. The wind tore at my shirt and raked its fingers through my hair. Rain soaked through my canvas shoes. I felt the squelch in them, and my toes had a hard time getting purchase.

I risked a look back at the helm, feeling a little alarmed at the wild angle of the deck. I saw my Amazonian husband standing braced at the tiller, in seventh heaven at braving the elements and with little thought for his pitiful crew member.

In the far distance, I saw the other two boats heading to our mutual rendezvous at Rogues Roost. As the elements increased to a frenzied pitch, I tried to rise above panic, and a little voice in my head said how thrilling it was to be so alive with nature.

It didn't work. I was sopping wet, windblown, and a little scared.

Finally, through sheets of rain, I saw the channel entrance to our destination. The boat came around in a wild jibe, and suddenly and overwhelmingly, we were inside the rocks in a calm channel.

I let out my breath slowly, but my fingers were loath to relax.

"Well done," Rick said. "Wasn't that great fun?"

I managed to hold my tongue as I squelched back to the cabin for dry clothes and, hopefully, a large rum. The cabin was in shambles in spite of our careful stowing, and I had to dig around to find clean, dry clothing. Not much could be done about my hair in rattails.

I did the best I could.

From the boats rafted alongside, I heard chatter of the other crews. Ice tinkled, and as I prepared to climb from our boat, words from the seaworthy wife of another captain rang out. "What an exhilarating sail. Wasn't it great when the wind got up? What a challenge to sail through that."

There they stood, in smart navy-and-white stripes and white deck shoes, dry and neatly coiffed.

There was I, emerging from my drowned-rat persona.

I smiled and graciously accepted a large dark rum. As I did, a glorious sun broke through the clouds.

TALES FROM THE BUCCANEER INN
FRANK LEAMAN

I've lived a long life, much of that time on and around the ocean. The sea can be both a harsh master and a great teacher. I've learned many lessons during that time, some from the experiences of others. Over thirty-five years ago, at our resort, the Buccaneer Inn, in Chester on Mahone Bay, we saw all sorts of human effort, finding meaning in some of it.

The Golden Path

He would sit in the tavern and laugh with the crowd. We were young and took things as they appeared. He was always generous, buying rounds of beer. But what did we know about other realities and lives people had led?

He had come to Chester, Nova Scotia, a year before, professing love for ocean scenery, boats, and all things nautical. Everyone has a past, and he told us of his life in the hard rock mines of Ontario and his need for a different life in the outdoors. He bought a Cape Island fishing boat from a local Tancook fisherman and fitted her out for living aboard.

We frequently saw him at local social events, like kitchen parties and family barbeques. He liked to be there. But if one looked close, he was selective. Being selective in one's company is fine unless it shows that one is avoiding exposure.

No, I didn't expect him to act like an older salmon coming back to his spawning ground! It was just an intuitive feeling that he was somehow uneasy.

Every once in a while, he gave the impression he was running low on money. He might divulge details of his working trips away to his closest confidants but said nothing to most. He would return to Chester after a short time and bunk down on *Ernest Hemingway VI*, his

Cape Island boat. Once again, lobsters would be boiled and steaks consumed with lots of black rum and boisterous company.

Then the problems began.

An opinion maker in the local drinking hole asked a question that seemed harmless. Did this man have a treasure buried somewhere?

This question seemed credible at the time because of rumours that the Oak Island treasure had been found. I well remembered the wildest of stories. One suggested ancient gold coins had been exchanged for a parcel of land although the trail turned cold when examined. A new rumour would take its place, such as one about a man known to be from an Oak Island crew who showed a golden idol to another in the tavern.

These things build. One night when the booze ran high, another "wise man" said that the treasure tales were true and one near to them would soon be revealed. After he said it, he noticed his companions looked at him like at a candy bar in a weight watcher's convention. He beat a quick retreat.

A few days later, it happened.

The police made an arrest of our local mystery man aboard the *Ernest Hemingway VI.* In the weeks and months that followed, it came out in the media that our local mystery sailor had in fact been a miner in the gold mines of northern Canada. While working as a transfer man, he had stolen a large bar of gold. In further confessions, he revealed that he kept this bar hidden on his boat and financed his lifestyle by sawing off pieces to sell during his time away from Chester.

This latest chicanery settled well with a group in the tavern. They laughed that, over the years when a bit of work was needed, an old coin, real but worth little, would be "found" on Oak Island. This would cause another dig and jobs for the locals.

When I ruminate back through the years, I recall all the different ways the stories developed. The vision of our miner with a hacksaw cutting off a piece of his gold bar to finance his lifestyle is thought provoking. In his case, the magician played one trick too many.

I know it has been asked if it ever gets cold on the moral high ground, but the actual path can get grey. People think it incredible that hard-headed business people would sacrifice money and time for treasure hunting. Just look at the record and watch the excitement and passion that appears when gold or a great fortune for the taking is mentioned. Over the years, I have seen many people become captured by thoughts of gold on Oak Island. Are these dreams in their heads or just stars in their eyes?

Escape from Death

They said Bruno had been to more parties than Captain Morgan! Don't fool with him, I was advised, but I was also told he could handle a boat in a rough dangerous sea.

I wanted to take our boat, the *Buccaneer Lady*, to Halifax from our lodge at Chester. We needed to go to Leckie's Nautical to get our compass adjusted by their man and purchase some supplies. We would be back that night. I knew it would be black along the coast, and although we had two Caterpillar diesels, it would be pushing it if anything went amiss.

The trip up to Halifax was perfect. We made Betty's Island, Sambro, and past Hen and Chickens to our destination. History shows judgement is very important, and my choice of Bruno seemed good. I began to relax.

The compass man from Leckie's took longer than we figured. After jigging and jogging around the harbour to known compass points, we found it was late in the day.

No matter because we had Bruno who was reported to be unbeatable.

Some drinking was going on but I felt it not extreme. I felt the tiredness of the day, and the wings of night, as they say, took me to my bunk for a lay down. I was more exhausted than I thought, and in a short time, I was in dreamland. Bruno and the others could take her to Mahone Bay and the Tancook Islands where they were to awaken me.

Rudely awakened by the mate who appeared drunk, I was taken to the bridge and a loud argument!

"Where do you say we are?" they cried.

I forced myself to reckon, and then I saw what they call the White Horses.

I shouted, "Turn her around, now! You have come in on the coast too soon. You are entering Horseshoe Reef, and the rocks and water spouts will deep six us fast."

Just then, a water spout reared up from the bottom and the wind blew spume everywhere. We turned the *Buccaneer Lady*, and through God's grace, we escaped to sea. Such a sobering effect I hadn't seen for years. They now saw their error, which would probably have killed us all.

It has been said some people are saved to save others, and I have seen this to be true many times. I also know that it isn't what you know that's dangerous, but what you think you know.

Dream Traveller

A dream of mankind is to find freedom and adventure in a perfect climate and culture. Of course, freedom usually carries huge responsibilities, and the Promised Land is always somewhere else.

Dreams are eternal, and in financial circles, promises of any number of panaceas are amply offered. Yachts that can sail the seven seas to exotic destinations are among the most common.

If the poor victim dared to ask, when shown the promoters' and brokers' yachts, "Where are the customers' yachts?" they would be somehow dismissed as too cautious.

One Toronto promoter dreamed up a plan to have a communal or condominium yacht.

What if a magic plan could be offered where one could sail to fantastic locations with a group of like-minded people and share costs and possibly duties when and where available? What if one could share ownership in a beautiful yacht and show some reward for one's daily grind? These kinds of heavy thoughts had always enticed mankind, and this time was no exception.

The magic carpet in this case was a seventy-foot sailing yacht painted bright red, called *Dream Traveller.*

After leaving Toronto to great fanfare, *Traveller* came down the great St. Lawrence River. After some sobering episodes, she arrived at a port in Prince Edward Island. At that destination, some of the more practical "owners" lost the scales over their eyes. They realized they were responsible for a very large sailboat's care and maintenance. A decision was made to continue to Chester, Nova Scotia.

By the time she reached Chester, we were introduced to a now diminished group. More reality set in, and while new problems were found, fate intervened in the form of a hurricane.

What happened then is still a matter of debate. Yes, the *Dream Traveller* broke loose from her fastenings and eventually foundered. It was now a question of who was looking after her. Who could or should have intervened?

Eventually what was left of the *Dream Traveller* was taken to sea and disposed of by sinking, and all was made ready for the next dream.

It has been said that those who don't believe in magic will never see it. I feel we should never give up on our dreams, and if our ship doesn't come in, we should go out and get one. But we must be willing to accept that all dreams come at a price.

The Buccaneer Lady *in Mahone Bay.*
The author is standing on the flying bridge.

LOST IN SHANGRI-LA
PAUL BOURGEOIS

"In shangri-la/ this kathmandu/ i am aware/ of objectives/ and subjectives/ but i still try/
to grow out of myself/ into this mythology/ i have built around me."
Into Myth, Kathmandu, /90

I have a window seat lifting off from Kathmandu airport, the ninth of April, 1990. Plane above the clouds, pillars stacked on a white landscape like temples. We turn from K2 and Everest towards Heathrow and then to Nova Scotia.

A clattering of glasses to my right shoulder.

"A whiskey," I tell the stewardess. "One piece of ice." She hands me a tiny bottle and a little cup. I pour the whiskey and place the drink on the tray before me.

Like this plane ride, the Buddhists believe this life is only a transition. We are passing through a confusing dream towards a reality we cannot know. But I have no memory of a time before my birth. I am dreaming I am a political dissident who has been involved in the writing of seditious material. My eyes close.

***

Danny Farmer waited on a threadbare couch in the lobby of the Friendly Home Guest House while a sixteen-year-old behind a tiny desk worked to organize a room for him.

A thin pale man with crazy eyes and a moustache too big for his dissipated body pulled himself next to Daniel.

"Are you an American?"

"I'm Canadian," Danny corrected him. He should have had flags sewn to his clothes and luggage to show people he wasn't American. "What are you?"

The moustachioed man's name was Gabriel. He was thirty-one, had been born in Iran, but when the Shah was overthrown he had been studying electronics in India. He'd received a letter from his family. "Don't come home. Don't ever come home." Gabriel had been without a country ever since, while his family stayed in Iran and died off one by one.

Over the months they stayed together, Gabriel taught Danny that anything was possible in Kathmandu. He'd helped him find a job at the Nepalese Language Institute, and they rented an apartment together up the hill, over one of the biggest momo shops in Kathmandu.

Gabriel wanted to go to Canada and was awaiting a decision from the United Nations on his refugee status. He checked the apartment constantly for hidden microphones, and he cried himself to sleep every night.

**

The Nepalese Language Institute was a large building near the corner of Dilli Bazaar and Puutalisadak, which became Bag Bazaar and turned onto the main drive, Durbar Marg, the main road full of banks and bookstores which led up to the King's Palace. The protesters would march up the thoroughfare shouting, "Democracy. Ha. Ha." And then they would read political speeches before the king's palace and police would come with clubs and haul them off to prison.

Daniel came into work as normal on Monday morning. Gabriel sat at a table in the middle of the room and the director, a short fat Nepalese Buddhist, stood by the plate-glass window, hands behind his back, rocking, looking down on barber shops, hole-in-the-wall cafés, kiosks where people bought pirated copies of Tracy Chapman's *Talking about a Revolution* and Living Colour's *Cult of Personality.* There was a line of people into a tiny shop across the street, waiting to get their passports copied.

The marches started on that street before they turned the corner onto Durbar Marg. Three police stood at the corner.

"Mr. Prakash has been taken for questioning," the director said. Mr. Prakash was an old Indian professor who had been teaching history at the institute. He wasn't expected to return. The director turned to Danny. "Do you carry your passport with you?"

"Usually," Danny replied.

"All the teachers here should have ID cards," the director instructed, "especially the foreign ones. If you are questioned, it's important the police know you are living and working in Nepal."

"I thought the foreigners were safe. The king didn't want to antagonize his money supply."

"The people have started firebombing tourist buses. The king can't hide the rebellion anymore. What are you doing today?"

"I have a meeting with a student in the afternoon."

"You can use the study room. Could you go across the street with Gabriel right now and have your picture taken? I have the cards ready."

***

Danny and Gabriel crossed the street, agitation in the air, brushing past bicycles and small motorized taxis, and ducked under a curtain into a small shop. They looked at the line of people waiting for passport photos, and they were there to get pictures for worker ID cards. Gabriel laughed.

"All these people want to leave Kathmandu and here you are trying so hard to stay."

A small boy took their money and blessed Ganesha, the elephant-headed god, which overlooked the cash register. A young man, glistening with dark sweat, T-shirt and shorts hanging from his body, took an instant camera from a small table and motioned for them to stand against a white screen.

Afterwards, Danny and Gabriel went up to the director's office. And then Danny waited to meet his student.

***

Knock, knock.

"Come in," Danny called from the study room. The student entered and Danny motioned for him to sit at the table with him.

He approached the desk with two ragged sheets of loose leaf and set them down before Danny.

The boy was a law student from the Government University. He sat down and looked hopefully across the table at Danny.

"I've already read this in Nepalese," the student explained. "I would like you to correct my English."

Danny nodded and took out his pencil. He pulled the papers towards him and read.

"We, the people of Nepal, demand the resignation of the king of Nepal... We demand that the single-party monarchy be disbanded... We demand a multi-party democracy be established... We demand the freedom of the political prisoners..."

Danny was silent for a while. He could imagine the students before the palace shouting their demands, tensions mounting, and then the tear gas and shooting and people scattering. He looked at the speech before him and then looked down at the police on the corner. They were demonstrating how to beat civilians and laughing.

"If those fellows down there knew what we had up here, it wouldn't be good for us, would it?"

The student shook his head. Danny took a deep breath.

"Okay," I said. "I'll do the best I can. But when you get this paper home, I want you to rewrite it all and burn anything with my handwriting."

***

The plane buffets. I wake momentarily and open my eyes. The seatbelt sign has come on. We are somewhere over Russia. I sip my drink, close my eyes, and go back to sleep.

BORDERTOWN
PAUL BOURGEOIS

I've set out to seek
redemption and acceptance
and make the strange places new.

Yesterday I
was lying on a dirty cot,
no sheets,
noises through the plywood walls
at night
with a radio and the battery running low,
the bus had just arrived.

Somewhere
between here and there
in a bordertown hotel,
a makeshift place
of broken sheds
and bars and midnight coffee houses
in the Himalayan foothills.
And I
drink chai,
that's tea with milk
in small cups
shaped from clay,
baked in manure
and made to throw away.

And yesterday I
was on the road
to Kathmandu

unsleeping in a grimy
bordertown hotel
betwixt India and Nepal
trying to catch the bus
because the trains don't run
in the mountains
where the roads are thin
between mountain and oblivion
and the busses have no doors,
the spotter hanging watching
wheels and earth and sky
while the young Buddhist driver
negotiates the pass,
secure that life is but
a bordertown
between birth and death.

BUTCHERSHOP IN KATHMANDU
PAUL BOURGEOIS

In butcher shops on hooks in Kathmandu
in early morning after Hindu-Buddhist prayers are said
thin dark men hang meat
of goats and water buffaloes
and lay down heads with staring eyes
on countertops and at the back
legs from chopped bodies stand against the walls
and entrails spread across the floor
from freshly slaughtered lives
and though I gather my Tibetan coat about my neck
the flesh still steams defiant of its own demise.

The nights are cold and I have leased a down-filled bag
and sleep alone inside a tiny hotel room
with thin and dirty papered peeling walls
and as my breath dissolves below my nose
I tuck my hands inside my sleeves to keep them warm
and watch the ducks and poultry
root through trash along the street
while Asian girls pour tea.
I want so much to share the world I hold inside my flesh
and realize that I, like meat, am only death
warmed over once by lust to give pretense.

WORLDS
TOM ROBSON

Reclining
On the private balcony of my not-quite luxurious hotel.
Spanish spring warm.
Comfortably tired.
Vacation-siesta-satisfied.
The memory of a morning stroll
Along the people-friendly, resort promenade,
Feeds the contentment of this holiday interlude.

> My eyes lift,
> From the escape pages of a vacation novel,
> To gaze across the busy street
> At a terrace balcony, with six apartment doors,
> Two floors below.
> This balcony, unlike mine, offers no view of an ocean
> Whose visible presence encourages exploration.

One door,
From a mid-balcony apartment, opens.
A worn, apprehensive face peeks out,
Checking both ways,
Eyeing the thirty meter stretch of walkway.
It is empty.
All is clear.

> The cane
> Followed by one hesitant foot after the other,
> Begins the short, shared-balcony walk.
> Shuffling steps, take her to one limit of her world.
> At this extremity, she turns and,

Perhaps fearing interlopers,
She quick, tip-tap-cane steps
To the other outer limit of her exploration.

Her refuge
The still open, apartment door.
Her one and only sideways glance
Is not out to the world beyond the railing,
To gaze up
To the Torremolinos' high rises and hills;
Or down
To the traffic and people-busy street.

    Instead
    She peeks back in through her own, open door.
    Seeming to fear that someone might have invaded her world
    In those brief moments when her back was turned.
    Into her home, she retreats.
    Once safe inside she turns,
    Sufficiently secure to check her outer space,
    Beyond the imprisoning balcony rail.

Briefly
Our gazes meet.
Her eyes pause and seem to lock on mine,
Suspicious that, two floors up,
And a street away,
I represent a potential security breach;
An alien threat to the privacy of her daily excursion.
Reassuringly I wave to her;

    Retreating
    Her silhouette, backlit,
    Framed in the shaded doorway,
    Does not permit me to read any facial reaction
    To my friendly overture.
    But the body language responds.
    A swift turn.
    The snap-bang closing of the door.

She seals off
Her inner world. Her refuge.
I imagine the clicks of the locks and bolts;
Each emphasizing
That I am an unwelcome observer
Of the bounds of her declining years.
The limitations of her journeys
And the security of her solitude.

    How far
    Had her youthful world stretched?
    It had to extend beyond the thirty meters
    Of that balcony, she shares.
    Perhaps, even now, it broadens
    And she moves through to the elevator-facing, inner door,
    Leading from her safe haven.
    Does she venture forth, through that exit, hidden from me?

How is it
That my aging life,
Sharing near as many years as hers,
Has brought me five million meters from my back door?
Why can I fearlessly explore places and people
In this new corner of my larger world?
Yet my innocent, friendly gesture poses such a threat.
That she beats a hasty retreat to the safety of her insular world?

FLIGHTS OF FANCY
WILMA STEWART-WHITE

This story is about women of "a certain age" who love to travel and observe all aspects of life en route. Having taken many similar trips to England and Europe to glorious gardens, these women are very familiar to me.

The ladies sat in a row, patiently waiting. They were very good at waiting, having had much experience throughout their lives. They had waited for husbands to come and go, and babies to come and grow. They had waited for small lives to become big lives. Now, most of their waiting was just for them. Their journeys were just beginning.

Each lady wore a nametag with a little watering can on it just to be sure everyone understood this was a garden tour group. They were nothing if not organized and seasoned travelers. They travelled with all the accoutrements for waiting—books, needlework, travel journals, guidebooks, and of course, garden magazines—so now a little wait for a plane was a mere trifle.

Many of them had travelled together before. The tour leader, Hilary, had greeted and introduced new and old with her usual unbounded enthusiasm and cheer. They were all fond of Hilary and shook their heads and smiled at her peccadilloes. Didn't she always get them there one way or another?

The three newcomers checked their itineraries, smiling and nodding at the row of watching ladies, who in turn smiled and nodded at them.

Agnes took out her bag of needlework and began stitching. It was something she could easily do without thinking, and it was very soothing. She wasn't at all sure about this trip. Travelling without a man for the first time would be difficult. Who would carry her suitcase and struggle with it at the luggage carousel? What about tipping and ordering drinks? Surely, she couldn't be expected to order her own? Who would deal with any unpleasantness—should that be Hilary?

Agnes had always had a long trail of husbands or partners and well knew the importance of being on the arm of a man who knew how to look after a lady such as herself. *We will see,* she thought, *we will see.* She bent her carefully coloured taupe-and-silver hair over her stitching.

Anne fussed over the contents of her purse and then, for good measure, the contents of her carry-on: ticket, passport, itinerary, money of all sorts. Would she ever be able to produce the right document on demand? Any kind of uniform frazzled her—policemen, customs officials, or dog catchers. They all inspired instant panic, and for no good reason, her fingers shook and her mind went blank. She wasn't, however, worried about the actual trip. She was sure she would be transported by the Gardens of England. Sissinghurst and Great Dixter had long been her companions as she turned the pages of her many gardening books. The delights unrolled in her mind, and she gave a small sigh of pleasure and anticipation.

Even though Ray had been dead and gone for over a year, she still hadn't grown accustomed to all this exhilarating freedom. No large shadow stood behind her, sternly correcting or criticizing. Life had indeed looked up.

Meg sat watching the row of ladies closely. What on Earth was she doing with a group of unknown ladies? She avoided ladies in clusters at church or book clubs or needlework groups. It didn't matter to her that they were all rigorously shunned. Here she was voluntarily going on tour with twenty-three total strangers except, of course, her long-time friend Hilary who had shoehorned her into this venture knowing her weakness for English gardens. Was she mad?

Her life had changed completely with the sudden death of her husband, and keeping her head above water was the best she could do. Her first instinct was to hide out in her dear little house by the bay and dig herself into oblivion in the garden, but Hilary and her children coaxed her into taking the trip. Like Anne, she had spent years mooning over delectable English vicarage gardens drowning in roses. So, she had succumbed. Neatly packed in her carryon was a brand-new camera with which she planned to capture England's "green and pleasant land." No one, she hoped, knew that she was petrified to fly over the ocean. She pulled out her new murder mystery but soon gave in to watching the row of garden tour ladies. They reminded her of a box of sugar almonds from her childhood: pale pastels all in a row, but as Meg remembered, the interiors were distinctive and of surprising substance. She was a person who loved mysteries, and she travelled with a whole cast of unknowns. This aspect alone would give the trip interest, and who knew what she might discover from her fellow travelers about their lives, loves, and dark secrets under the almond-tinted outfits.

The airport around them was noisy and very busy. Flights came and went, and there was much to watch. Hilary frowned when a further delay was announced. The ladies, however, were content to wait and watch the swirling crowds and the mini-dramas around them. Indeed, one very obligingly began right across from them.

A tall, handsome grey-haired man appeared, well-dressed in a dinner jacket. He carried a black bag and a curious box. He looked around with a slightly worried air, selected a spot, and set out his belongings. Immediately, the ladies sat up and adjusted themselves accordingly, fluffing their hair and settling their scarves. They watched with great interest.

The box opened into a small table. This he covered with a crisp white cloth. From the bag, he took a slender vase with a single dark red rose and set it on the table. What next, they wondered. Was he a magician preparing a trick? They exchanged glances.

Two crystal flutes appeared and a bottle of champagne. With practiced aplomb, he eased out the cork and carefully filled the glasses. Agnes remembered many such glasses poured for her. Anne recalled movies with just such handsome men. Meg, with a burst of memory, felt the tiny bubbles prick her tongue.

He sat behind the table and faced the arrival doors, as did the entire row of ladies. Would this mystery unfold before they left?

Suddenly, their flight was called. What a dilemma! How could they leave amid this drama? Moving slowly, they gathered their belongings. Hilary urged them to the gate, but she too wished to see what would happen. The double doors swung open and passengers streamed through from an arriving flight. The gentleman stood. The ladies hovered.

From the crowd emerged a tall, elegant woman with grey hair pulled into a careless chignon and wrapped in a glorious shawl. Catching sight of the man, she paused. The crowd eddied around her. He stood arms outstretched, waiting. They faced each other, motionless. Passersby sensed the drama unfolding. The ladies, en route to their plane, craned their necks to catch a final glimpse as Hilary shooed them down the ramp. They could only imagine the conclusion of this drama and would happily spend the next six hours doing so.

The flight to Heathrow taxied and slowly lifted off. Glorious sun broke through the clouds.

A BOX OF TROUBLE
PHIL YEATS

The trouble began when Robert and Kathleen Melville visited the recently opened Canadian Museum of Immigration at Pier 21 on the Halifax waterfront. It had a different name in those days, but it was the same museum celebrating the arrival of a million people who entered Canada through the immigration warehouses.

Near the end of their visit, Kathleen stopped at the room with passenger lists and other information about ships arriving between the 1920s and the 1970s.

"We should take a moment to find the records for your mother's ship. You do know when she arrived, don't you?"

She must have understood his reluctance to delve into his family history and noticed he hurried by this exhibit on the way in. But now, she couldn't resist a little genealogical research.

"Yeah, spring of 1946," Kathleen's husband of twenty-five years replied. "She came on a ship bringing war brides from Britain. But really, I think we should give this a miss."

"Oh, come on. You should know something about your parents, even if it's only the date your mother arrived and the name of her ship."

Her persistence didn't surprise him. She had intimate knowledge of the lives of dozens of her relatives going back several generations. She found his lack of family history bizarre.

Robert followed her into the room and stood aside while she attacked the available information.

"This cannot be!" she exclaimed after discovering the records were incomplete. "Thousands of women and children entered Canada through this facility in 1946 and '47. They must have arrivals from the spring of '46."

"I'm sure they do, but it's crowded today, and this place just opened. On a quieter day, someone could probably find the records for you."

"No, Robert, I won't be dissuaded," she said, tapping her forefinger on the museum brochure. "It says right here the records are computerized and accessible."

"Fine, but it also says their database is a work in progress with much of the information not yet entered. Years ago, Aunt Edith gave me a box of information about my parents. Perhaps it has something that would help narrow your search and allow you to return with a more specific question."

Aunt Edith was Robert's closest relative and the only "parent" he'd known. He immediately regretted mentioning the box she gave him before he and Kathleen married. Kathleen's eyes lit up, and from that moment, nothing would stop her. She delved into his family history, and in the process, opened a Pandora's Box of problems that took years to resolve.

Robert heard nothing about the box, or his mother's story, for several weeks. Then, one morning at breakfast, it was back on the table.

"This box has lots of information about your father, but almost nothing about your mother," Kathleen said, dropping the tattered old cardboard box on the table with a thump. "It doesn't help tie down her trip to Canada or anything else."

"Oh, well," he said with a shrug. "It was worth a try. And it's not like this whole problem is that important."

"But it is important! The box has stuff from your father's high school and documents and photos from his RCAF pilot training at a base in Manitoba. There are wartime photos from 1942 and 1943 in England. Then, there's a big gap until his plane crash in 1946, his hospitalization in England, and his return to Canada. It has the official records and several medals. But only a few photos of your mother with your father in a wheelchair from the winter of 1946/47. Then nothing until the summer when we have a few baby pictures of you with your mother, but many more with your father and aunt."

She stopped abruptly and Robert waited for her to continue.

"That's more or less the story Aunt Edith told me," he said when Kathleen remained silent. "He joined the RCAF in '41, went to the UK in '42, and stayed on after VE day to ferry people and supplies to the ongoing war in Asia. In the fall of '45, he contributed to the decommissioning of the war effort. The plane crash occurred in December '45. He received one of the medals for saving the life of a big wig on the crippled plane he crash-landed."

"But what about your mother?"

"They met in England, got married in the summer of 1945, and had an apartment near his base. After his injury, they arranged for my mother to come over on one of those war bride ships. I'm sure Aunt Edith told me it was the spring of 1946, so consistent with when he was repatriated."

"But why is there nothing in this damned box?"

He sighed. "Two reasons. First, Dad's family didn't approve of the marriage, so not a lot of happy family photos got preserved. Second, my mother would have had any documents or photos from their time in England. Who knows what *she* did with them."

"What about your mother's life here in Canada? Why aren't there photos of you with your mother after the summer of 1947?"

"Why do you insist on pursuing this?" Robert asked. It was painful ancient history he'd rather forget, but he knew Kathleen wouldn't quit. "My mother left just months after I was born, and I don't know where she went. It was different for my father. He was happy with a son but incapable of looking after me. Aunt Edith looked after both of us until he died in 1949 from lingering effects of the plane crash. Then she was my guardian until I went to university. End of story. There's nothing else to tell."

***

Kathleen realized Robert wasn't happy discussing his past. She stopped badgering him after he failed to answer questions about his grandparents' reaction and whether anyone tried to find his mother. During the ensuing months, however, she continued her search with her usual doggedness tackling thorny problems.

One Saturday morning late in the fall, she presented Robert with the fruits of her labours. She produced timelines for activities from 1945 to 1949, one for his mother, one for his father, and one for him. His mother's timeline contained a bombshell.

"Are you sure?" he asked, pointing at her date for his mother's arrival in Canada.

"Yes, I'm sure. I have the date for their wedding, their address in the UK, and details of her trip to Canada. She arrived in Halifax on the Queen Mary on the third of October, 1946. Her name is on the passenger list at the museum."

The implication was obvious. Robert's birthdate of the twenty-third of June, 1947, meant conception in September 1946 in England. His father wasn't his father.

Remaining aloof from Kathleen's investigation was no longer an option. Robert stood beside her as she attacked the problem with increased vigour. Kathleen focused her efforts on the twelve male officers who were passengers on the September crossing of the Queen Mary and soon zeroed in on one Reginald MacNaughton.

"Why focus on those twelve?" Robert asked. "My real father could have been any of thousands of English men. We cannot narrow down the date of conception to that crossing."

"No, we can't, but I'm guessing she abandoned you to be with her lover. There's no indication she returned to Britain, so a paramour who came from England to Canada at the same time is our best bet. If we don't focus on them, the scope of our problem expands massively. Until we eliminate them, we should target that dozen. Then, if necessary, we can broaden our search."

"I suppose that makes sense. But why have you highlighted this one guy, Captain MacNaughton?"

Kathleen opened a manila file folder and shuffled through the contents.

"Because of this," she said, waving a small envelope she'd extracted from the file. "It was in the box Aunt Edith gave you. No letter, but the timing's right. It's addressed to your mother at your grandparents' home and has a return address. Guess who?"

Robert sighed. "Captain MacNaughton, I presume."

"Exactly. Captain Reginald MacNaughton and an address in Westmount."

"Westmount. That's the fanciest neighbourhood in Montreal. Did you locate the house on Google maps?"

"I did. A huge mansion that must be worth a fortune. He was young, and he'd just come home from the war, so he was unlikely to have such a big place. It must be his parents' house, but I haven't confirmed it."

"Let's assume it belongs, or belonged, to his family. There's now a link between my mother and MacNaughton, but it could be anything, correspondence related to an event on their trip across the pond, for example."

"But it's a link, and we can investigate what it might mean."

"Okay, but go carefully. We don't want to ruffle feathers digging into innocent history."

During the following weeks, they discovered that Reginald MacNaughton was the third son of a wealthy Montreal family. In 1950, he married Liana Williams in a civil ceremony.

"Williams," Robert said. "That was my mother's maiden name but her first name was Mary. I wonder what her middle name was."

"Elizabeth. That's what her birth record said, Mary Elizabeth Williams. Her mother's name was also Mary, Mary Helen. All I have for Liana Williams is the marriage announcement in the newspaper. The name in any official record may be different."

"Williams is a common name; it must be the third or fourth most common one here and in England. But what about Liana? What's its origin? Is it a diminutive form of Elizabeth?"

Kathleen shook her head. "I looked that up. It is related to Elizabeth, but no suggestion it's a diminutive."

"Hard to imagine my mother chose after she left my father to go by her middle name but changed it from Elizabeth to Liana."

"Not an easy link, but possible. I found newspaper photographs of Liana MacNaughton in the early 1950s."

Kathleen laid four photos of Liana MacNaughton on the table beside ones she had for Mary Melville.

"Okay," Robert said after inspecting the handful of old black and white photos. "They're both on the short side and have light-coloured hair, but from these grainy photos, can we really say anything else? They could be the same person or two different ones."

***

Over the next months, Robert and Kathleen continued their investigation when time allowed but came up with no new leads after efforts to contact the MacNaughton family were rebuffed. Their enthusiasm waned, and other tasks, including shepherding their three children through the final years of high school and on to university, took precedence. They shelved the search for the identity of Robert's father and what happened to his mother.

In the summer of 2009, ten years after their first visit to the immigration museum, a phone call changed everything.

"My name is Mary MacNaughton," the caller said. "I'm trying to locate a Mr. Robert Melville who grew up in Lachine, Quebec, in the 1950s and 1960s."

"That's my name, and I did grow up in Lachine during that time," Robert replied after a slight hesitation.

"Then you must be my half-brother," Mary replied, her voice bubbling with enthusiasm.

"Slow down. We need to be sure before we set ourselves up for a major disappointment. I'm Robert James Melville, and my aunt, Edith Melville, raised me. Are we still on the right track?"

"Yes. Our mother's maiden name was Mary Elizabeth Williams, but everyone called her Liana. Our father's name was Reginald Stewart MacNaughton. We didn't know she had a previous marriage."

"So, are you phoning to tell me she died?" Robert asked.

"Please, don't get me wrong. We, my brothers and I, had no idea we had an older brother until after she died. It was in her will and a big surprise to us."

"And what does your father say?"

"He died several years ago. He split his fortune between our mother and his three legitimate children. But, Mother, she included you and your children in her will."

"And that's why you're phoning?"

"Partly. Mr. Milton, the family lawyer, will look after the details. I learned all this yesterday and decided to contact you. One doesn't learn she has an older half-brother every day. I had to get in touch."

"Right. Well, it's a shock, but as you say, an extraordinary event. Let's wait until I get the details. Then if everything goes well, we can talk again. Kathleen, my wife, will be delighted I've finally found my family."

They exchanged contact information before ending the call. Robert went away saddened because once again, he'd have to address his mixed feelings about being an illegitimate son. And how would Mary and her three brothers react when they learned they were true siblings?

But mostly, he wondered what Kathleen would say when she learned she'd been right about Captain Reginald MacNaughton. That is, after she said "I told you so." She would say that before anything else.

Various missives from Mr. Milton arrived over the next few weeks. The final one contained a sealed letter from Robert's mother.

Dear Robert,

When you receive this letter, I will no longer be alive. The family lawyer will have informed you of the relevant details of my life and the inheritance I provided for you and your children. I wish to explain why I left my husband, James Melville, and abandoned you, my six-month-old baby.

I should start in 1944. Reggie MacNaughton and I were engaged to be married, and shortly before a big RAF raid on the twenty-fourth of

March, we made love, the only time we did during the war. Reggie's plane was lost on that raid. We had no news of him, and it was assumed he died in the crash. I was left alone and pregnant with no family to turn to because they died during the blitz.

James Melville became my anchor during this time, comforting me when we learned that Reggie, my lover and his close friend, had been lost. When my pregnancy started to show, he married me. I lost the baby. It wasn't James' baby, but he took the loss harder than I did. He was kind and gentle, and we stayed reasonably happily married until December 1945 when his plane crashed. He survived, but was very badly hurt and not expected to live more than a few months. He was repatriated to Canada in the spring of 1946, and in September, I got a berth on the Queen Mary, one of the ships carrying Canadian war brides to Halifax.

When I arrived at the dock in Southampton two days before the ship sailed, one of the first people I saw was Reggie MacNaughton. There he was as fit and dapper as ever, the same old devil-may-care charmer I'd been in love with two years earlier. No explanation of how he survived or why he hadn't been in touch. Nothing. He was just there and swept me off my feet like he had when we first met. And he was taking the same ship home to Canada.

By the time we arrived in Halifax, I was pregnant again, and you were born the following June. James wasn't expected to live very long. In fact, I wasn't sure he'd be alive when I reached Montreal. Reggie and I agreed we would wait until James died, then get married.

We didn't know I was pregnant, and that changed everything. Reggie rejected any thought of accepting you; it wouldn't fit in with his strict Scottish Presbyterian family. After you were born, he put pressure on me to abandon you and James, and continue with our plan to marry after James died.

I acquiesced six months after you were born. It is a terrible thing for a woman to leave her husband, and a mother to leave her child, but that is what I did. I feared Reggie would abandon me. I had to choose you or Reggie, and I chose Reggie. I accept that you will never understand how I could leave you behind, but it was a different world back then. James' family knew he wasn't your father. They wouldn't have stood by me after he died. We would have been alone in a world that was very hard on single mothers and their children. Reggie offered me love and security, and I could only hope his family would eventually accept you.

We were married in 1950 after James died, but Reggie never relented in his refusal to let me have any contact with you. But I knew Edith was good to you, and I did manage to keep track. You are married with three grown children, and you have all done well. I wish I could have been in touch, but it wasn't to be until Reggie died in 2007. But then I was too old and frail, and I'd left it too long. I was bedridden, and all I could do was write this letter.

I don't ask for forgiveness, just that you understand my motivation.

Goodbye, my son I never knew. I hope you and your family live long, prosperous, healthy lives.

The letter simply ended. It wasn't even signed.

The front door opened while Robert stared at the letter, uncertain what to think. Kathleen entered, encumbered by parcels from a shopping trip. She took one look at Robert and exclaimed, "What's wrong?"

Robert passed her the letter and retreated to the kitchen to make tea. This, he decided as he swirled boiling water in the pot, must be something he inherited from his mother. He always reached for the teapot during a crisis. Kathleen didn't, nor did Aunt Edith. It had to result from his English heritage.

A few minutes later, he carried a tray with a teapot, two cups, and a small pitcher of milk into the living room. "What do you think?" he asked Kathleen.

"It shows we were right about your father's identity and explains several things we didn't understand. More than anything else, it shows us your father was a rogue."

Robert thought the letter also suggested his mother hoped to become pregnant when she found Reggie again. It looked like both his parents may have been rogues.

This story is fictional but inspired by a real event. My mother was a British war bride who entered Canada through the immigration warehouses at Pier 21 just after the end of World War II. She was surprisingly reluctant to visit the Canadian Museum of Immigration when she visited Halifax approximately fifty years later. Her reluctance made me wonder how many of these immigrant stories might have elements of intrigue.

Canadian Museum of Immigration, Pier 21, Halifax, Nova Scotia.

MYSTERY, MYSTICISM, OR JUST ME?
JUDI RISSER

I attended a master's program with the University of Glasgow as an international student in the fall of 2014. I had difficulty adjusting to the program and finally confided this to a kindly English professor. Yes, he wore a tweed jacket with elbow patches. When he suggested that I go to the mountain, I told him I preferred the water. "I am from Nova Scotia," I babbled between sighs and sobs. He kindly suggested I go to the Isle of Arran.

I had no idea what to expect. At that time, I struggled and needed space, a quiet place to think, to find clarity. I had to re-evaluate what I was doing in Scotland. Was I really headed on the right path? I thought this was an unusual suggestion, but I hurried back to my flat, searched online where exactly the Isle of Arran was and what train I needed to take to get to the ferry. I learned that the island was the seventh largest island in Scotland. Its nickname was "Miniature Scotland" because it had the same geological features as Scotland with the Highlands and Lowlands.

The island was still one of the most famous places in determining the age of the earth. In 1787, James Hutton, a scientist working on a theory to determine the age of the earth, visited the island, near Lochranza, and used information from the area.

As I stood at the bow of the ferry, I was awed by the vision of the island ahead. The sun glowing through the cloud cover was breathtaking. It seemed magical. I felt lighter the closer we came.

The ferry landed late. It was dark. I had made no reservations before running out to catch the train. It took a little while, but I did find a nice B&B just outside the small town centre. The next morning, the owner of the B&B made me a huge Scottish breakfast. Could Scottish breakfasts be made any other way?

While I ate enough to feed a family of four, she suggested the many things I could do on the island. She told me about Brodick Castle just up the road, within walking distance from the B&B. My ears perked at the fact that there were ancient standing stones right on the island. I had been in Scotland for two months and had yet to see anything of that nature.

I packed a few things for my adventure and walked across the road to the water. As I strolled along a beautiful beach, I could see the castle grounds up in the distance, with Goatfell Mountain behind it.

Brodick Castle had a turbulent history, dating back to when the Vikings likely used the site defensively until they were driven from the island. Brodick was actually "old Norse" for broad bay.

After meandering through beautifully tended gardens, I followed a path into the woods to a fence. It was early morning, and no one was around except two Highland cows, one white, the other brown. Such unusual creatures. Long shaggy hair, looking like a cross between a bison and a cow. They were only mildly curious as to who the intruder might be. I leaned against the post for a while and admired the lush green fields, mountains, and ever-changing skies.

Scotland did have the most amazing skies, often layered in thick billowy mounds, streams of white and gold sunlight filtering through. And, more times than I could count, I often experienced threatening moments of ominous black just before bursts of rain! But, in a moment, it was over; the sun shone brilliantly until the next white tufts approached. And, it began again; wild patterns, or no patterns, building to magnificence, only to climax, once again. And, so it began again, within the blink of an eye!

As I walked out of the wooded area past the castle, I followed the trail down to the main road. I wondered at all the different vegetation, large palm trees, enormous fungi shaped like conch shells, rhododendrons, and amazing colours everywhere, even though it was November. Apparently, the air was quite warm all year round on the island, influenced by the warm Gulf Stream waters, protecting and nourishing the abundant vegetation.

It didn't take long before the bus showed up. I hopped on and bought the "day ticket" where I could get on and off as many times as I liked. I told the bus driver what I was looking for and was dropped off on the other side of the island. Before I got off the bus, the driver pointed towards acres and acres of sheep pastures and said in a very strong accent, "That way." Although I could see nothing beyond the sheep pastures, I sensed something amazing awaited me over the horizon.

Not a soul in sight. With every step forward, I felt like I walked back in time. I walked for a long time. You know how it feels? How it seems to take forever to get to a place one's never been before? It felt like that. Partly due to my excitement and partly due to apprehension of travelling alone in an unknown place. "Normal people don't do stuff like this, do they?" I thought aloud.

Then, I came across short stones in oddly formed groupings. I won't lie, after reading the *Outlander*, not once but twice, I was a bit shocked. I expected the stones to be bigger. I thought it was just too anti-climactic, so I forged on. The pastures, the scenery was just so breathtaking. My excitement mounted.

I kept walking past sheep and more sheep. Past the Moss Farm ruins. I would always remember how the tree grew out of the building. My reaction was that this place had been expanding beyond all limits. There was a moment when I thought this was what the world would look like when we were all gone. This place was truly timeless...

And then, I saw them! Several free-standing sandstone slabs, over five metres high! Awe! Delight!

I cried...

I sat on an overturned stone for a long time. I finally felt at peace. I imagined what sorts of events, celebrations, and activities might have taken place at these massive stone groupings centuries ago or even, back in the mists of time.

Then, I thought about Claire, the heroine of the *Outlander*... Could we really slip back into time?

How fascinating it would be to time travel. It was then, at that very moment, I felt as if I could have been sitting on that fallen stone centuries before. There were no people, nothing that revealed what century it was, other than me, my clothing, my thoughts, and my memories. Oddly mystical. Oddly familiar.

And then I pondered, *Can one find clarity in still more mystery?*

Sometimes, I wonder at the mysterious fascination I have with Scotland. Where does it come from? I have wanted to go there for as long as I can remember. I feel so comfortable there, I fear nothing. In some ways, it feels just like home. Geographically, energetically, spiritually. Perhaps, that is why I was born in "New Scotland" or Nova Scotia, in this lifetime. And here, in this mysterious place tucked into the Isle of Arran, I feel a subtle shift... this time, in me.

My adventure to Suide Choir Fhionn or Fingal's Cauldron Seat,
Isle of Arran.

ON THE BACK ROADS OF ENGLAND AND WALES
JANET DOLEMAN

This was our third time in the UK, and having already toured many of the guidebook hotspots on earlier trips, my husband and I were ready to hit the back roads with cameras and notebooks, to experience our own version of Great Britain. These brief snapshots capture only a sampling of the picturesque and mythical sights of Cornwall, pastoral and historical gems of middle England and South Wales, and the distant secrets of the North York Moors and Yorkshire coast. Stories are plentiful to come across in an ancient storied land, and we believe that new stories unfolded around us along every path and byway.

Unseasonably sunny dry weather coincided with our three weeks in England and Wales in September 2014. At long last, we were on the road to Cornwall! Previous schedules hadn't allowed adequate time to travel all the way to the "toe" of England. Having spent hours with my nose in novels by famous authors such as Daphne du Maurier and Rosamunde Pilcher, among others, we were finally here, heading into the west-of-England sunset on the wrong side of the road. Cornwall in the sun was a jewel box of delights: green-blue sea, white surf, stone and pastel-tinted houses overlooking tiny harbours, white (at a distance) sheep and black-and-white "Belties" cattle dotting rocky green pastures. The typical damp, misty English weather was nowhere to be found. At Land's End, the horizon was limitless; as we stood high above the rollicking North Atlantic, it felt exactly like its name, the end of the world.

We'd decided to explore Tintagel of King Arthur lore, the stark ruins of abandoned tin mines, fish 'n chip shops, Cornish pasties, and Port Isaac (made famous as the fictional "Portwenn" in the TV series *Doc Martin*). The more we researched, the thicker became our itinerary: St. Michael's Mount, a twin to Mont St. Michel on the coast of France, and who could miss Penzance and the narrow seaside streets of St. Ives? An unexpected additional attraction appeared when we pulled into the courtyard of the "Countryman of Trink" Inn on the outskirts of St. Ives, to find a white van in the drive displaying an Elvis Presley silhouette and website address. Robert "Elvis" and Sylvia Wilkinson keep an immaculate, comfortable establishment: old exterior, updated interior, with a tiny brook trickling through their property and cattle lowing nearby. He cooks a great fish 'n chips meal, does "Elvis," and occasionally dashes off to perform at shows in nearby towns.

***

Britain is crisscrossed by thousands of rivers and canals; one of the most tranquil has to be the shallow stream meandering through the small, quaint Cotswold village of Bourton-on-the-Water. Resident ducks and swans paddle lazily beneath old humpback stone bridges, a purely English backdrop to swarms of tourists tramping back and forth to sample the pub fare and shop wares. It was there in our cozy third-floor room tucked under the eaves of Chestnuts B&B that we fell asleep on the night of the Scottish referendum, the eighteenth of September, 2014, not knowing when we awoke the following morning whether Scotland would be still attached or if there would be a giant gap beyond the northern borders. The previous day's *Times* was clad in the Union flag (Union Jack, commonly), and the words "D-Day for the Union," plus a quotation by Robert Burns in 1788: "Should auld acquaintance be forgot, and never brought to mind? Should auld acquaintance be forgot, and auld lang syne?"

Outside our skylight, the sky brightened with the rising sun, wood pigeons cooed, and tour buses jostled for position along the high street. The ducks and swans paraded in their tidy stream. It was business as usual in the breakfast room: two American tourists, a couple from Essex and two Canadians devouring plates of "full English breakfasts." Scotland had voted "NO" to independence. The world went on as before in this little village well south of the border.

***

The renowned waterway, the Kennet and Avon canal, runs through the town of Newbury in Berkshire, where we'd booked a hotel room in order to visit nearby Highclere Castle (*Downton Abbey*). We'd purchased tickets online months before; the entrance was timed for early afternoon, giving us a few hours to explore the streets and shops of Newbury. We'd arrived the evening before, and a relaxing walk through the centre of town prompted my husband to grab his camera and capture lighted reflections on the canal's surface. We popped into Morrison's for the *Times* and a cold drink to take back to our hotel room.

"Did you hear they're shooting scenes for the new *Star Wars* movie outside of town, by Greenham Common?" one clerk said to the other. "My son's mate John was up flying the other day and spotted the set."

The clerk cheerfully sorted our coins and took the appropriate amount. "Where're you from?" asked the taller lady, when my husband spoke, betraying his non-British accent. As soon as he said "Canada," both women were quick to tell us about a friend of a friend in Canada, in Toronto perhaps, or was it Alberta?

The next morning after a glorious breakfast in a café/bakery, my husband sat outside on a bench, camera on his lap, waiting for me to emerge from a shop called "Temptation" (aptly named). An elderly man approached and asked if he was photographing the town on assignment. When we explained we were visiting from Canada, he quietly stated, "I was almost a Canadian," and began to tell us his story.

"It was during the war. I was all ready to leave, dressed in my coat and hat, with my suitcase in hand and a note pinned to my coat. I was one of a shipload of child evacuees ready to sail on the next ship bound for Canada. Only I never got to go. The ship ahead of ours was torpedoed and sunk.[1] Almost everyone died, so they cancelled our sailing and there I was."

He grew up in England, and eventually, at age eighty-four, he did get to go to Canada, first to Toronto, then on to Calgary, and all the way west to Vancouver.

Shoppers brushed past us as we listened intently to his story. His courteous, sincere demeanour captured our attention, standing there on a cobbled sidewalk with English morning sunshine on our heads, not at all in a hurry.

***

We were intent on exploring walking trails in the southern reaches of the Brecon Beacons National Park in South Wales. What better British

---

[1] *Later, research pointed to the ill-fated ship as the SS* City of Benares.

sort of thing to do in such fine weather. Printed guide brochure in hand, we laced up our shoes, grabbed our day packs, and set off down the trail. A rough wooden sign painted with unintelligible Welsh words met us at the end of a concrete footbridge. Partially obscured by grass and weeds below was the English translation warning visitors of the deep cold water in the grotto-like ravine, one of the attractions on the Four Waterfalls Walk. We carefully ascended the far bank, the path crisscrossed by exposed tree roots and loose stones, with a perilous drop to the riverbed on our right. Two Welsh ladies out for an afternoon's walk paused for a break, and so we met Dawn and Norma. Dawn, the younger of the two, admitted to having walked to the summit of Mt. Snowdon in North Wales, a feat that would be described as mountain climbing in our part of the world.

Farther along the trail, all of us descended a steep stone and mud staircase to the river, where we were rewarded by a close-up view of *Sgwd-yr-Eira* ("falls of snow") waterfall. Agile walkers balanced on slippery rocks behind the falls, amongst them a young couple intent on capturing themselves on camera. A man waded into the stream to set up a tripod for his camera equipment; his friend was more inclined to talk, explaining that the recent dry weather had caused the waterfall to be greatly reduced from its usual volume. He told us his passion was photographing church interiors, and as he and my husband exchanged photography tips, I guessed that he would have plenty of subject matter to keep him occupied for months, if not years.

Climbing back up to the main trail, with only a couple of pauses to catch our breath, we relaxed on a sturdy wooden trailside bench in the sun and delved into our knapsacks for sandwiches, reflecting on the joy of a moment's rest deep in the Welsh countryside. Returning to our vehicle in the car park, we passed by sheep unfazed by two more humans tromping by their lunch room. It was as if we'd emerged from a parallel world shrouded in leafy green shadows, punctuated by the sounds of tumbling water over stones into rock pools, and by our footsteps following time-worn tracks through overgrown pastures.

***

A burbling brook ran behind our self-catering cottage near Pontardawe in South Wales, the only other sound at night besides the soft baa-ing of sheep across the lane. Converted from a former stable, the upstairs windows of the quaint and spacious cottage overlooked an enticing property on the other side of a high stone wall. A stately manor house sat amid sweeping lawns, statuary, ornamental pond and fountain, the flood-lit château-like façade presenting a fascinating vision. Once part of the estate but now completely separate from the working sheep farm and cottage-rental business, our host informed us it was listed at 1.9 million pounds. I relished the idea of viewing the opulence sure to be found within its walls but suspected that only serious prospective buyers would be granted tours of the interior.

Instead, on the advice of a local councillor we'd met at a local pub the night before, we ventured beyond the grand estate *Plas Cilybybell* (our mangled pronunciation had been duly corrected) to the ancient parish church. Founded in the Diocese of Llandaff, it boasts the second oldest ringing bell in Wales. A newly-painted sign in the forecourt proclaimed "its font is medieval, the tower is Norman and the congregation is friendly and welcoming," a description not commonly found in our comparatively young country of Canada. Although fascinated by the long history of this country church and wondering whether our waterfall friend had photographed it yet, we still faced several hours' drive to visit our friends in Thirsk. We reluctantly left the wild and beautiful Welsh landscapes to follow the dual carriageways east and north.

One of the highlights and necessary components of our trips to Great Britain was visiting friends in Thirsk, North Yorkshire, known also as James Herriot country. My father had served with the RCAF during WWII, stationed at RAF Leeming, near Northallerton and Ripon. During his time there, he and his fellow airmen were befriended by local families, as so many soldiers were. It was from one particular acquaintance that a closer friendship grew and from that a bond that lasted for over sixty years, cultivated by trans-Atlantic letters and a yearly Yorkshire calendar at Christmas. It is a link that first drew us there to meet this older couple in 2008, but only after my own parents had passed away, regretfully. We have established our own bond now, progressing from cards and letters to emails and online photo-sharing. And, yes, we've renewed the calendar exchange between our families.

More adventures awaited, since every corner of this compact but intriguing land yielded mysteries and treasures, from Whitby on the North Sea coast, which is said to have inspired Bram Stoker's *Dracula*, to a tiny town further inland below the North York Moors, where the *Mouseman of Kilburn* began a craftsman tradition. Ancient King Arthur lore and *Elvis* in Cornwall, *Star Wars* sightings and WWII stories: our journey continued to fascinate, with pages of pencilled notes to add to a future itinerary, definitely another year to return to put our own stamp on "discovering Britain."

THE END (or the beginning....)

A JOURNEY IN TIME
JANET MCGINITY

During a month in France in November 2014, we were astounded at the kindness of our newfound French cousins, who welcomed us to the land of our ancestors and even invited us to a meal in their home.

"**W**e prepared a little circuit and will see you tomorrow," announced the email from our French contact. I turned to my husband Peter. "It's not very clear. They might drop off a map, expecting us to rent a car and explore on our own, or maybe they'll take us somewhere."

We had arrived by train that November afternoon of 2014 in the city of Poitiers, in central France, for the last two days of a month-long visit to the country. We were eager to learn about the origin of our families' histories. Both Peter's and my ancestors were Acadians, who emigrated in the 1640s from small villages north of Poitiers.

Before leaving Canada, I contacted a former colleague, who ran a tour company centred on Acadian themes here and in France. I asked him if he could put us in touch with French people in that area from whom we might learn about our Acadian origins. He did so and provided email addresses. One was a history buff, the other a curator of an Acadian genealogy centre. We contacted them both.

The next morning, we waited outside our hotel. A black Peugeot pulled over, and a man stepped out.

"Are you Janet and Peter? I am Alain Bourreau, and this is my wife, Claudie." He gestured for us to climb in.

They took us first to Archigny, a tiny village along the Acadian Line. Eight houses remained of a scheme to resettle several hundred Acadians deported back to France in the 1760s. These people had lived as refugees in the city of Chatellereault for ten years. A local lord got the idea of settling them to farm his property. But the land was poor, and most of the settlers left not long after. One house had been restored as a museum. The curator was a descendant of those who stayed.

Our hosts then drove to Chatellereault, near their own home, pointing out a New Brunswick Street and a Grand Pre Place where the refugees had lived. We wanted to take them to a brasserie for lunch, our treat, but they refused.

"You will come to our house," Alain said with a smile.

At their home, Alain poured us glasses of Pineau de Charentes, a local aperitif wine. For lunch, Claudie brought us first a sliced baguette with butter, black radishes, and country pate; then a pork tenderloin with apples and potatoes; salad; a dish of beans cooked with sausage; a Poitou cookie with a crackly top; a plate of local goat cheeses, followed by coffee and then offered chocolate! The conversation flowed in English and French throughout the three-hour lunch, helped by glasses of wine.

Alain, Claudie, and I compared words for common things in the Poitevin dialect and my Acadian dialect. They were nearly always the same.

"Janet, you speak Poitevin!" he exclaimed.

"No," I said. "YOU speak the dialect of most Acadians in the Maritimes." We looked at each other. Suddenly, the four centuries that separated us from France had evaporated.

Alain said, "Ah, we must go. It's nearly four p.m., and we have more places to visit."

He took us to nearby Derce, a tiny village with a thousand-year-old church; then to Monts-sur-Guesnes, a village with a performing arts centre.

A blond woman came to greet us at the door. She was Michele Touret, the curator of the Acadian genealogy centre whom we had emailed and arranged to visit the following day. She introduced us as two visiting Acadians, and we rose to applause from the audience.

The play was *La Sagouine,* featuring an Acadian washerwoman with a salty tongue. The one hundred or so people in the audience understood the dialect spoken in eastern New Brunswick by author Antonine Maillet. They laughed quietly, in all the right places.

After the play, people besieged us with questions. We learned that some Acadians had Berber blood, an inheritance of the Moors who fought the French in the Battle of Poitiers in 832. Apparently Moorish women, perhaps camp followers, intermarried with French people after the battle, since a mitochondrial DNA test done on other Acadians had shown this connection.

Later, Alain and Claudie took us to a restaurant on the outskirts of Loudun. We shared a gala dinner with our hosts and others involved in the play or supporters of the Acadian Museum. We made firm friends and have stayed in contact.

Around eleven p.m., Alain and Claudie took us back to Poitiers to our hotel. And so ended the "little circuit" and so started a warm friendship, which continues to this day via email. We call ourselves "Les Cousins," The Cousins.

An Acadian farm of the 1770s in France (now a museum).

AN EVENING IN PARIS
PHIL YEATS

Scott Flynn arrived at Paris' Gare Montparnasse during a warm, sunny July afternoon in 1979. The heat was a welcome change after two weeks of cold, foggy weather on a small oceanographic vessel in the Bay of Biscay. Severe weather had slowed progress and swallowed up the three contingency days in their plans. After docking, he only had time to oversee packing of their gear before hopping a train from Saint Nazaire to Paris. The gale-force winds had blown away thoughts of days touring the countryside.

Before he left, his French hosts warned Scott of a one-day baggage-handlers strike affecting flights departing Charles de Gaulle Airport. They assured him the latest of the all-too-frequent work actions by French unions would cause chaos for one day, but not affect his flight the next morning. Doubting their optimism, he'd pared his luggage to a few essential items in a backpack. Everything else would be shipped home with the sampling gear.

After days cooped up on an uncomfortable vessel, the twenty-six-year-old oceanographer relished a walk through the streets of one of Europe's scenic cities. He didn't have time to visit major tourist attractions but hoped to find somewhere informal for a before-dinner drink. After a relaxing meal, he could take a late-evening train to his airport hotel.

Scott strolled along Rue des Rennes, a long narrow street with ornate three-storey buildings crowding the road on either side. He admired the elegance of Parisian women as he sauntered down the street. Across the broad tree-lined Boulevard Saint-Germain, Rue des Rennes merged with Rue Bonaparte, an even narrower street that led to the River Seine.

On the north side of the river, Scott passed the entrance to the Louvre where hordes of tourists queued in the late-afternoon sun. In the adjacent Jardin des Tuileries, he admired dozens of sculptures, some by famous artists like Rodin. But time was passing, and he headed to the Paris offices of Air Canada to check on the strike situation before finding somewhere for dinner.

A crowd outside a hotel housing offices of an American airline caught his attention. He stopped, thinking he might learn about the strike without the worry of reaching the Air Canada office before it closed.

He noticed her immediately after entering the airline office. She was of above-average height, with straight shoulder-length flaxen hair. She looked trendy in low-cut flared jeans and midriff-baring tube top in coordinating shades of blue under a loose-fitting short-sleeved white over-blouse with a large sunburst of yellow. The blouse was open except for a tie near the bottom. She displayed the carefree chic of an American co-ed rather than the elegance of a French woman.

The worried look on her face spoiled her sexy appearance. Her brow was furrowed, and she absentmindedly bit the knuckle of her thumb as she watched messages scrolling across a mechanized notice board.

As Scott stood behind her, she turned and smiled weakly. "Are you in the same position as me?"

He looked away from the moving letters. "I should be okay. My flight doesn't leave until late tomorrow morning. What about you? Were you leaving today and caught up in the foolishness?"

"I arrived at the airport this morning and should have been most of the way home by now. But the whole place was in turmoil with no flights leaving. They offered me a room for the night and a promise of a flight tomorrow. At least that gave me a place to stash my stuff."

"And you've had an extra day to visit Paris."

"But I'm worried about getting out tomorrow and the problems I might have if I don't get home."

"So, you returned here hoping to get an update."

"Yeah, I visited the Jeu de Paume museum, so it hasn't been a total waste. Do you know the place? It's in the Tuilleries Garden, only a short distance from here."

He smiled. The Tuilleries Garden was one of his favourite Paris landmarks. "I walked through the garden this afternoon admiring the statues. I didn't have time for the museum, but I've been there before. What was your favourite thing?"

"Manet's *Luncheon on the Grass*. What was it supposed to mean?"

"I remember that one. I think it was a scene from the Bois de Boulogne, a place where people went for assignations."

"But she's naked. The two guys are sitting there discussing something and ignoring her."

"If I remember correctly, another naked woman is in the background. I think it's about romantic attachments."

"I still think it's odd. But what did you like when you toured the museum?"

"The small bronze statues by Degas. I don't remember if I saw them there or somewhere else, but of all the impressionist stuff, I like them best."

"They're controversial, aren't they?"

"Because there are masses of copies, some only trinkets for tourists?"

"Yeah, they're like Salvador Dali's, so many fakes it demeans the real ones."

"I don't care. I'd love to have my own Degas statue of a naked ballet dancer, even if it's only a copy and not even full size."

She sighed. "Having famous art is just a dream, isn't it? People like us will have nothing but copies and prints."

"Perhaps, but we can enjoy this last evening in Paris. That is if you don't have something else to do?"

"Are you inviting me out for the evening?"

"I guess. I'm planning to find an outdoor café for a beer or a glass of wine, then somewhere for dinner. There may even be time for entertainment before I make my way to the airport. If you want to share that with me, I'd be delighted."

"Really? I've been having a terrible time shaking off the idea I'm stuck in limbo. Having someone to distract me would be great."

He shrugged his shoulders. "What's there to worry about? No flights are leaving until tomorrow morning, so you might as well enjoy the time you have."

"But all afternoon I worried the airport would open, flights would leave, and I'd be left behind."

Scott smiled and shook his head. "That's not happening, so where should we go for dinner?"

"Pigalle or Montmartre, you know, the bohemian sector. And my name's Brenda. What's yours?"

"Scott, and I doubt if we'd get in anywhere famous like the Moulin Rouge. But the district isn't far from here, so we could wander around and sit somewhere sipping wine and pretending we're French intellectuals or artists."

"But I don't speak French or have an artist's beret."

They headed toward Place Pigalle and the Boulevard de Clichy, two strangers brought together by chance. As they strolled along Rue Jean Baptiste Pigalle, Scott watched for a store selling berets, a common item for French shops catering to tourists. He found one near a café with tables along the sidewalk.

He steered Brenda into the shop and its shelf of berets. They found one that fit perfectly and coordinated with the colours in her outfit. While he queued to pay for it, she wandered amongst other items on display.

A few minutes later, Scott stood on the pavement waiting for Brenda. She emerged from the shop, carrying a large plasticized craft paper bag with handles. An object wrapped in tissue paper protruded from it.

Brenda pounced on an empty table in front of the busy café as another couple stood to leave. Scott smiled, thinking he wouldn't have been quick enough if snagging the table had been left to him. She placed her bag with its mysterious contents in one chair and arranged two other chairs close together against the wall of the café. She patted one, beckoning Scott to join her, where they could relax watching Parisians going about their daily lives.

Neither said anything until the waiter arrived with a glass of white wine for Brenda and a draught beer for Scott.

"Wonderful," Brenda sighed. "This is the first time I've been able to relax with someone and watch the world go by."

"You've not been having a good time during your visit?"

"I've been here three days and seen lots of things. But I'm on my own, so relaxing at a café or going to a nightclub hasn't seemed like a good idea."

"Other than the Jeu de Paume, where have you been?"

"All the normal things. The Eiffel Tower, the Louvre, Notre Dame, Sacre Coeur."

"So, you've already been to Montmartre."

"But only during the day. I didn't linger like this or dare come by myself at night."

"If you're worried, why did you come to Paris on your own?"

"I came for my best friend's wedding. We graduated from college this spring. She's from Austria and went home to get married. The ceremony was five days ago in Vienna, and before that, we had a wonderful week together. After the wedding, I came here on my own. It hasn't, you know, been as good because I've been too timid."

"Too bad you didn't have someone to enjoy it with you."

"Yeah, right. I hoped my boyfriend would join me, but we've only been together for a few months, and he hardly knew my friend. And it costs a lot, so he decided not to come. But what about you? How did you end up here escorting me around the racier parts of Paris?"

Scott laughed as he glanced at their surroundings. "Doesn't look like a particularly racy spot."

"Maybe not, but tell me about yourself."

"What's to tell? The engineering company I work for does environmental work and surveys of oceanic conditions. An oil company hired us to make measurements in the Bay of Biscay. Three colleagues and I spent the last ten days on a small ship. I hoped to be a tourist for a few days after the expedition, but the weather was rotten, and we didn't get finished until yesterday. So I came here today, and tomorrow, I fly home to Halifax."

"What happened to your three colleagues? Why aren't they with you?"

"They rented a car and left this morning for a week touring God knows where."

"But you didn't go with them?"

"No. I'm getting married in two weeks. It didn't seem appropriate to be taking time off with the guys."

"And your fiancée didn't want to meet you here?"

"The wedding was set before we got the job, so the timing wasn't good. Anyway, we spent three weeks together in Europe last summer and have other plans for our honeymoon."

Brenda put her hand on top of Scott's, the first time they'd touched. "We're both in serious relationships, but we can still have a good time together without, you know, doing anything we'll feel guilty about, can't we?"

She smiled and looked toward the street. Scott wasn't sure about the wistful tone of her voice. Was she uncertain about her relationship and saddened to learn that Scott was unlikely to be interested in anything untoward?

They'd finished their drinks, so Scott put money on the table and stood.

"How do you know how much to leave?" Brenda asked.

"He left a chit when he brought our drinks, and the prices are posted on the wall behind you."

"And that's enough for both of us?" she asked as she gathered her parcel and adjusted her new beret.

He nodded.

"Well, thank you. I didn't mean for you to buy me hats and pay for my drinks."

"Don't be silly. It's the least I can do. Let's see if we can find somewhere for dinner on the way to the Moulin Rouge. We won't be able to get in, but we can watch the action outside. And later, we can find a smaller club or theatre for an hour or two before making our way to the airport."

After an unpretentious dinner, they ventured deeper into the Pigalle district. On a side street, a man with white face paint, wearing a mime's traditional black trousers with suspenders and striped black-and-white T-shirt, accosted them. Without saying a word, he passed Brenda a sheet of paper and pointed to the door of a theatre.

Brenda scanned the page before turning to Scott. "Should we? It's, you know, all done in mime, so it shouldn't matter that I don't understand French."

The play started when a woman with a mime's white face paint half-dragged and half-carried a large wooden sandwich board down the left-hand side of the stage. At first, Scott thought she was naked, but as she struggled with the oversized board using a mime's exaggerated gestures, he realized she wore a skin-coloured leotard. Words in French gave an abbreviated explanation of the first scene. After fussing to get the sandwich board arranged exactly right, she perched gargoyle-like as three actors entered from the back.

One was the young man who'd been on the street soliciting audience members. The second was another young actor distinguished by maroon rather than black trousers. The third cast member was a young woman, also in whiteface, wearing the stereotypical black-and-white T-shirt. But instead of trousers, she wore black tights and a short burgundy miniskirt.

The series of sandwich boards the nearly naked "narrator" dragged to the front of the stage helped the audience understand the play. She would drag one down the right-hand side and set it up. Then she would saunter across the stage front to collect the one on the left and drag it to the exit. A few minutes later, she would repeat the process, positioning a new board on the left and removing the one on the right. The boards outlined the plot as the three actors mimed a typical love-triangle romance. During the hour-long play, the young woman threw over the man in the black trousers in favour of the one in maroon. The details, for Scott and Brenda, were lost in translation.

Brenda dozed with her head on Scott's shoulder on the train to their airport hotel and waited while he checked in.

"What floor?" she asked as they stepped into the elevator.

"Sixth," he replied. "Same as yours, is it not?"

She stopped in front of her door and placed the parcel she'd been carrying on the floor as she searched for her key. She turned to him once she found it.

"Thank you for a most enjoyable afternoon and evening. You've turned what was a sad visit to Paris into one I'll always remember. But it's late and I must get up early, so..." She reached up and gave Scott a passionate kiss with her arms around his neck, not the formal little thank you kiss on the cheek he expected. After what seemed like ages, she retrieved the object wrapped in tissue paper.

"This is for you," she said before disappearing into her room.

Scott stood with the package in his hands after the door clicked shut. He waited until he heard her engage the lock before proceeding to his own room to unwrap the package. He knew he would find a replica of a Degas bronze.

In the morning, he looked for her as he ate a solitary breakfast and made his way to the terminal's international departures area. He didn't find her.

***

Twenty-seven years later, Scott Flynn strolled into the lobby of his Toronto hotel after a meeting of his environmental engineering firm's upper-management team. He noticed her immediately.

The same woman, older and more conservatively dressed, but unmistakably the one he'd spent several hours with in Paris so many years earlier. Brenda stood near the reception desk with the same worried look on her face as she bit on the knuckle of her right thumb and stared at an electronic message board.

"What's the matter?" he asked. "Have they cancelled your flight?"

She turned and gaped. "Oh, my God, Scott, is it really you? You look as wonderful as you did—"

"Me. I'm getting old and grey, but you, you're as young and beautiful as you were in 1979."

"Oh, dear. Has it been that long?" she asked, glancing around. "Can we go somewhere to talk? I feel weak, like I might collapse."

He led her to one of the lobby's sofas. She smiled and took his hand in hers. She'd clearly forgotten whatever had been worrying her seconds earlier.

"If I remember right, you were on your way home to get married," she said.

"We were happily married for twenty-five years and raised two daughters. One is married and working in the investment world, and the other is in university."

"But you said were."

"Sarah died two years ago. Cancer. What about you? You were going home to a steamy romance."

Brenda sighed. "Not so steamy, and it didn't work out as well as yours. But tonight, could we relive our evening in Paris, have a drink at a street-side bar, dinner somewhere and, you know, catch up?"

"Even if it is only stodgy old Toronto," Scott added as he helped her to her feet.

Later that evening, they returned to the hotel. Their rooms, by chance, were once again on the same floor. When they arrived at her door, she invited him in.

This story is fictional but inspired by a real event. Like many other travellers, I was trapped by a work stoppage at the Paris airport in the 1970s. I had dinner with a fellow traveller at an airport hotel restaurant that was overwhelmed by the sudden influx of customers. Later, I wondered about romantic attachments that could have been generated by such chance encounters.

Edgar Degas, The Spanish Dance, Ackland Art Museum, Chapel Hill, North Carolina.Ⓒ

JOURNEY'S END

STRAW PEOPLE
CATHERINE A. MACKENZIE

"Hey, kiddos, wanna hear a story?"

Aunty G huffed and puffed into my bedroom where my brother, Steven, and I sat on the floor playing Monopoly. Even had her floppy, fluffy, fake rabbit-fur slippers been soundless on the carpet, she announced her presence with her laboured breathing.

Steven and I dropped our game pieces. "Yes! Yes!"

She leaned toward us and whispered, "You ain't real siblings. Ain't real at all." She stuck a bony finger into my cheek. "And you, little missy, ain't legit."

I strained to hear and ignored spittle spraying my face. "Legit?"

She looked at me first and then at Steven. "Your mother ain't your mother. She ain't who you think she is. Ain't so high and mighty just 'cause she goes to church every Sunday. She's a sinner. Her past will haunt you, mark my words."

Aunty G wheezed and coughed before rambling further, but I heard nothing else. Steven and I weren't brother and sister? I was illegitimate? And Mom? What was Aunty G saying about my mother? I'd always been closer to Dad than Mom. Was that a sign? Was Mom forced to love us or put on a show to keep our father's love?

I raced downstairs and into the parlour where my parents sat quietly. With my hands on my hips, I shouted, "Who are my parents? My real parents?"

Mom dropped her book.

Dad made a funny noise in his throat and scratched his chin as he always did before a serious discussion. "What brought this on?"

I glared at my father. "Aunty G told me and Steven that Mom isn't our real mother. That we're not real brother and sister."

Dad glanced at Mom, whose face had turned scarlet. For several too-long minutes, he remained silent, and then he sighed. "I guess you're old enough to know." He hesitated, rubbing his eyes as if he'd just awakened, and sighed again. "Steven's mother died when he was born. Your mother," Dad patted Mom's leg, "adopted him after we married. But I'm your father and your mother is your mother."

"Mom is my mother but not Steven's?"

"Exactly."

"So, Aunty G was right? We're not real brother and sister?"

"Of course you are."

"But Aunty G said I was illegitimate."

Mom looked at Dad before saying, "I'm your mother, Susan." I detected a tear in her eye.

"Yes, she's your mother and I'm your father. That's all you need to know."

My heart thundered in my chest. Mom wasn't Steven's mother, but she was mine?

"I don't want to discuss this again. And ignore Aunty G. She doesn't know what she says," Dad said.

"But you're my real dad? And Steven's real dad?"

"I am." Dad stood and brushed the tear from my cheek. "Steven is too young to know about his biological mother, so let's keep this our secret, okay?"

"When will you tell Steven?"

Dad pondered for a few seconds. "When he's your age. Thirteen's a good age to know, right?"

I wasn't sure. Perhaps Steven would be happier thinking Mom was his real mother. "But Aunty G says I'm not real. Why would she say that?"

"Drat that drunken woman! She lives in the past, an old woman of regrets. Of course you're real. What a stupid question. Pinch yourself."

When I hesitated, Dad pinched my upper arm.

"Ow, that hurts." I glared at him.

Dad laughed. "See? You're real. You're spirited, healthy, and happy. That's all that matters."

I sauntered back to my room, where Steven sat alone on the floor. One of Aunty G's too-big pink slippers lay beside him as if she had evaporated or ran fast away before the boogieman could get her. Or the monster that caught those who lie?

Perhaps I was another big-mouth Aunty G, for I blabbed to Steven what Dad had said. Steven acted unconcerned. Maybe he was too young to comprehend my words. Or maybe he just didn't care. Despite that, we stood before the full-length mirror, trying to find resemblances—a minute detail to tie us together. I examined my face and pointed to a freckle. "There's that. And you have one, too."

"A freckle? Everyone has freckles."

"But what else is there? Your skin is darker than mine. Your eyes are darker, too."

"Our hair," Steven blurted. "We both have straight hair."

"Ya, but yours is brown. Mine is blonde."

"Yours is yellow. Mine is light brown. Pretty close. And your hair is like Mom's."

"I'm not sure she's my mother. I think they're lying. Something doesn't add up." Aunty G's word "illegitimate" burned in my mind. Why would she say that if it wasn't true?

I peered closer in the mirror. "Do we even look like Dad?"

"We're too young to look like him. He's old. When we're older, I'll look just like him. We're men, you know." Ten-year-old Steven stood taller as if that made him a man.

***

Aunty G, Dad's father's sister, was really Gertrude Grace Bennett. She never married nor had children of her own, so when Dad's mother died young, Gertrude became his surrogate mother.

Her words "not real" resonated with me for many years, and when I was younger, I had mulled over the meaning. If not real, were Steven and I fictional? We grew up together. Weren't we real since we breathed, suffered, and laughed?

When Aunty G was in her eighties, Dad convinced her to move from her apartment to Stonebrooke Home, where she'd have companionship and less stress. He felt so beholden to her that he brought her to our home on weekends and holidays. Since liquor wasn't permitted at Stonebrooke, he allowed her a stash at our house, and as soon as she'd consumed dinner, she'd drag out the amber-filled bottle. Although he agreed with Mom that liquor was a magnet pulling Aunty G to our home, he shrugged off her drinking habits.

Aunty G hated Stonebrooke and complained about lumps: lumps in her food, lumps in her bed. Oversized clothing camouflaging an obviously sizeable body made me view her as a life-sized lump.

When I was fifteen, she left Stonebrooke and came to live with us. The first day, she went off on a drunken tangent at the dinner table. "I tell ya, incest ain't right. And children born out of wedlock ain't right." Aunty G eyed Mom who glowered at Dad.

"Watch your language, Aunt Gertrude. Children are present." Dad sounded mad.

My head swivelled from Aunty G to my parents and back to her.

Steven had often jumped into my bed at night, and we would snuggle under the covers. If we had a flashlight, we read or played tent. Other times, we talked, comforted by the nearness of each other. When the hall floor creaked under our parents' footsteps, we watched the light shine through the partially open door. If one of them neared my room, the last one down the hall, a shadow entered first, which prompted Steven to slip down the far side of the bed and slide underneath—a frequent scenario that had taken place several times with neither Dad nor Mom the wiser. Once I discovered the meaning of incest, I no longer wanted him in my bed, but I missed our closeness, especially after Aunty G's rant.

How had Aunty G known Steven and I cuddled in my bed? Did Mom and Dad know, too? Did they think we had done "it?" That had happened years previously. How could blabber-guts Aunty G have kept a secret that long?

Mom glared at Dad again before leaving the room. Dad raced upstairs after her. Aunty G leaned back in the wooden chair, snickered, and poured another drink. Steven remained preoccupied with his food.

I snuck after my parents and listened outside their bedroom door. The door was ajar, and Mom sat on the bed with Dad's arm around her, his fingers kneading her upper arm.

Tears streamed down Mom's face. "God forgive me, but she needs to keep her mouth shut. All that talk of me not being their mother. It's upsetting the kids. And today was the last straw. Susan's acting like I don't love her, and you allow your aunt to get away with everything, like a spoiled child."

Dad dropped his arm and sighed. "She's almost ninety. She's not right in the head. The kids don't know what she's talking about."

Mom huffed. "You don't know what the kids know or don't know. You could take away the booze. Her lips might not be so loose then. A woman her age shouldn't be drinking anyhow. At least she's semi-sane when sober."

"She's set in her ways. She'd die if I restricted her drinking."

Mom didn't give up. "I'm afraid the kids will become alcoholics. And I'm positive she gets up in the middle of the night for swigs. And her words are horrid. Just horrid."

Dad kissed her on the cheek. "Ignore her. She likes to push your buttons. The kids know she drinks too much and talks nonsense. Besides, what do kids know?"

I called Mom "Ruby" a few times, especially when I got mad over a punishment, more to rebel than anything. Despite Steven's adoption and Mom and Dad's denials, I felt like the odd one. Were there more secrets? Was Steven not his dead mother's son? Scenarios crept through my mind.

Mom wouldn't elaborate on Aunty G's words, and Dad became annoyed if asked. Until Aunty G opened her blubbery mouth, Steven and I had thought Mom—Ruby—was our biological mother. Thanks to Aunty G, had Dad concocted a tale? Or had he told the truth?

One day, Dad came into my room. He gazed out the window for a few minutes until he spoke in a harsh tone. "Every time you question me or Mom, you disrespect your mother. Your real mother, the mother who is here now, alive in the flesh. I won't speak of this matter again. Understand? And don't ever call her Ruby again."

I stared at the spinning carpet, wanting to disappear beneath it where I used to hide boogers in the dark of night after picking my nose until it was clean and empty.

***

I entered Great Aunt Gertrude's room. Her eyes, wide open, stared at the ceiling. A few seconds passed before I clued in. I screamed, and Ruby—Mom—bounded into the room. One look and she knew.

She gathered me into her arms. "It's okay, sweetie. Don't cry."

I couldn't help it. I had never seen a dead person before, but mostly I cried for answers that had died with her. Aunty G had been bedridden for much of that year. A woman from town who had tended to her needs probably knew more than I.

After the funeral, while mourners congregated in the stifling hall, devouring teeny sandwiches and sweets and drinking ice-cold lemonade to beat the heat, Steven and I huddled in a corner. "What now?" I asked. "Who will tell us our answers?"

Steven whispered, "Maybe there's no answers. Did you ever think of that? Maybe Dad told the truth. Aunty G was a nutcase, you know."

I didn't answer.

Life progressed. Mom became our "real" mother again, and Steven and I were once again "real" siblings.

Mom and Dad seemed happier than ever. Was the demise of Aunty G and the burial of secrets the reason?

***

Seventeen-year-old Steven bounded into the kitchen. "Hurry." Tears streaked down his red face. "Help! They're after me."

I dropped the dishtowel. "Who's after you?"

"Mr. Hornberger. He's coming. With his shotgun." Steven flailed his arms and hopped about the room. "I have to hide. Where can I hide?"

Mom and Dad had gone into town, which left me in charge, and I deemed the situation serious. Ordinary hiding places like under the bed or in the closet wouldn't suffice.

I grabbed a straw. "Outside. Come on." I bolted through the back door, Steven at my feet. I stopped at the barn and pointed to the rain barrel. "Jump in."

Steven's face turned white. "What? It's full of water. I'll drown."

I held out the straw, and his face relaxed. I helped him in. Cold water splashed over me. He dunked below the surface, the straw pointing to dark clouds.

The situation escalated quickly. An enraged Mr. Hornberger and his oldest son, hefty Colin, emerged from the side of the house. I walked toward them, distancing myself from the barrel.

Mr. Hornberger's head swivelled back and forth. "Where is he? I know he's here."

"Who?"

"Your damned brother, that's who."

"Steven?"

"You have more than one?"

"No."

"Then it's Steven. Quit being the fool that you are."

Colin twirled a monstrous axe, like a weightless pencil, at his side. Mr. Hornberger brandished a rifle. "Let me at him. I swear to God I'm gonna kill him."

"He's not here."

"He's here. I smell your fear. And rightly so."

My stomach lurched, and I stepped back. I screeched, but the nearest neighbours, the rest of the Hornberger clan, wouldn't be of assistance even if they had heard me. When Colin raised the axe, I motioned behind me. "In the woods."

They advanced toward me. And then the water gurgled. All eyes fixated on bubbles emerging from the overflowing barrel.

Colin heaved the axe, aiming it at the middle of the barrel. Instead, the blade hit the rim with a great crunch, splitting the ancient wood down the side like a sharp knife slicing a tomato. Out tumbled Steven.

Dazed for several seconds, as were the Hornbergers, he regained his senses and tore into the woods, the Hornbergers charging after him.

Hunter and prey disappeared between the trees. I hoped my brother had the sense to shimmy up a tree. He excelled at gymnastics, but the hunters, bigger and stronger, would prevail; they always did.

While I wondered what to do, Mom and Dad returned. I had barely explained the situation when the Hornbergers reappeared, dragging Steven like a deer carcass.

I screamed.

Dad lunged at them. "Let him go."

They dropped Steven's arms. Covered in dirt, Steven remained on his back, his chest heaving.

"He done knocked up my Isabelle." Mr. Hornberger's spittle flew.

"Calm down," Dad said to the Hornbergers before yanking Steven to his feet.

Dad's forehead wrinkled, and his eyes blazed. "Is that right, son?"

Steven stared at the ground. Tears plopped to his feet. "I don't know."

Mr. Hornberger rammed the end of the rifle into the soil. "That's what my Issy says. She never lies."

Phooey, I thought.

The Bennetts and Hornbergers had never been the best of friends, but we'd been neighbourly. They thought us too hoity-toity, probably 'cause Dad had been to college; we thought them too hillbilly. Two such diverse cultures would never meet in the middle.

And now this.

And why hadn't Steven confided in me?

"Son?" Dad repeated.

"I don't know, Dad." Steven blubbered liked a beached whale. "We may have done it once—or tried to."

Dad flushed. "I don't need details."

The Hornbergers loomed before us as if waiting to pounce.

"Come into the house," Dad said. "Let's talk."

Mr. Hornberger's eyes flared, and he jabbed the rifle into the dirt again. "We don't need no talking. And if'n we do, it can be done right here."

Defeated, Dad shrugged. "My son will do what's right, won't you, son?"

Steven, without raising his head, mumbled. "Yes, Dad."

Mr. Hornberger raised his rifle. "No, not what you're thinking. No Hornberger will ever marry a Bennett. Us Hornbergers take care of our own."

And with those words, Mr. Hornberger and Colin stomped off.

Isabelle Hornberger was shipped to Vermont to live with relatives until the baby's birth. The plan, from what I had figured, was for her to give up the baby for adoption and return to Millville, Nova Scotia, as if nothing had happened.

Out of sight, out of mind, and we erased her from our lives. Since she never returned to town, the task was easy.

The subject wasn't discussed again, and the Hornbergers and the Bennetts never again spoke. We avoided each other if we happened upon them in town, and at town meetings or events, we sat on opposite sides of the room.

***

After Mom and Dad passed, Steven and I were alone. Life happened and passed us by. Neither of us married. The small community of Millville must have thought us incestuous, for we remained together in the family home. Perhaps they thought us as loony as Aunty G.

Steven was unconcerned. "It's the old kids' saying: sticks and stones and all that. We know the truth."

Did we? Our snuggling in bed flashed before me. We weren't teenagers then, and our parents hadn't yet discussed the birds and bees. We hadn't known those experiences were anything but two loving, innocent siblings.

Dad had been the first Bennett to attend college. Steven and I were supposed to have had better educations than he, but Steven wanted to be an auto mechanic and completed a two-year course at Millville Community College. I had no interest in college and secured a secretarial job at Kramer's Warehouse, a kilometre from our house.

Steven achieved his dream of opening his own auto shop, which he did on our property. Before his death, Dad had advanced him funds for

130

the building. The business started small, but soon Steven was overwhelmed with work. Dad would have been proud had he lived to see Steven's success.

One day, a visitor appeared at the front door. A young woman in her early twenties peered down at me from stilettos. "Is Steven Bennett home?"

She emitted an air of seriousness. Politeness didn't permit me to ask what she wanted, but I sensed she wasn't in need of an auto mechanic. I pointed to the dirt road alongside our driveway, noticing the fancy sports car parked in front of the house. "He's out back."

"Thanks."

When the shimmering red car disappeared down the lane, I lingered out of sight on the back porch. She stopped in front of the auto shop, pulled down the rear-view mirror, and adjusted her hair before exiting.

I sneaked across the yard and peeked through the open side window, where I had a good view of the two of them.

"I'm Cynthia, your granddaughter," the woman said.

I almost fainted. Steven frowned. He had no clue. *It's Isabelle's granddaughter*, I wanted to yell. *Your granddaughter!*

"Isabelle Hornberger was my grandmother."

Steven dropped the wrench. He stared at her for several seconds. "I see."

She broke the silence. "Don't worry. I don't want anything from you. I live in Vermont. Just here for a few days, checking out my roots."

Steven remained silent.

"Genealogy is the new fad, didn't you know?"

"No, I didn't."

"Everyone wants to know where they came from. Even celebrities."

How true, I thought, still not having resolved my parentage. Nice that she could. And nice that celebrities could. She, of course, referred to the popular television show *Who Do You Think You Are?* I had thought the show a bit of a farce and didn't believe for a second the show portrayed the truth. Then again, with celebrities' fortunes, they could hire anyone and everyone to research their pasts. What about us lowly folk left floundering? Life wasn't at all fair.

"I suppose," he said.

Would Cynthia's unexpected appearance prod Steven's interest in his biological mother? Everyone we loved was gone, and though it had been years since my curiosity had piqued, my desire for answers had never waned.

Cynthia examined his face. "I don't think we look anything alike, do we?"

"I'm not great at that sort of stuff, but no, I don't see a resemblance."

"Mind if I take a picture?" She withdrew a camera from her purse. "Mom might like to see what you look like."

Poor Steven, who hated to have his picture taken, didn't have a clue how to get out of the predicament. "Okay." His mouth formed a funny, fake grin; she clicked.

"I must go."

Steven's face crinkled. "That's it?"

"Yes, just wanted to see you."

"Okay. Ah... if you need your car worked on before you go, let me know."

She laughed. "My car's fine. It's brand new." She pointed at the open door.

"Porsche. Nice."

"Yes, isn't it gorgeous? Must go. Dinner with long-lost family tonight."

Steven brushed grey hair from his forehead, leaving a strip of grease across his weathered skin. "Perhaps I'll see you again."

"I doubt it. This is my first and last trip here. Not really my cuppa tea, know what I mean?"

Steven nodded. Did he know what she meant? Little Miss Hoity-toity was more hoity-toity than we'd ever been.

When she turned, I ducked. I slithered to the side of the building and watched her speed down the lane, dirt flying everywhere.

I giggled. The car's shine would be gone when she reached her destination.

***

Had the reunion between father and granddaughter been more amicable, Cynthia might have lingered around, enabling me to glean pointers on how to proceed in my parentage quest. Because of her sudden appearance—and disappearance—the nagging uncertainty that had plagued and perplexed me since Dad had closed the subject struck me like a barrage of bullets from Mr. Hornberger's rifle.

Who do you think you are?

The truth hit me—or, rather, the questions. I was older than my brother, and my parents married after his birth, so how could my supposed Mom—Ruby—be my mother? My head spun with flashbacks and falsehoods.

Steven's granddaughter had found her past. Shouldn't I? But I hadn't a clue how or where to begin.

Steven was still uninterested. He had believed Dad's explanation. "My biological mother lived and died having me. That's all I need to know. Dad and Mom will always be my parents."

"But I need to know about *me*," I said, selfishly emphasizing the "me."

"Dad told you the truth. What more do you want?"

I regretted allowing people to pass on without demanding answers, but our parents had taught us to respect elders—to be seen and not heard, most times not even seen, stored away like winter coats stuffed in the closet at springtime.

The most logical place to start was with my birth certificate, which I hadn't seen for a coon's age since I hadn't had any use for it. I didn't travel so had no need for a passport, and I'd never needed it for a marriage licence. I hadn't yet turned sixty-five. Would I need it for Canada pension? Had Mom and Dad kept our birth certificates from Steven and me for a reason? If the documents had been needed for school, neither of us had handled them.

Dad, a stickler for paperwork, stashed anything of importance into a metal box in the linen closet. After placing Dad's and Mom's death certificates in the box, I had placed it on the shelving unit in the parlour.

I delved into the box. The information on my birth certificate appeared correct, but why did Steven's certificate show his parents' names when mine didn't? Vernon Thomas Bennett was listed as Steven's father, and Dad's first wife, Augusta Jane Simmons, the woman rarely spoken of, was shown as Steven's mother.

Why were my parents' names omitted?

Nothing jumped at me from other papers in the box. How I wished answers could magically appear. Was Dad, even in death, controlling information?

My place of birth was Halifax. Would I have to travel two hours from Millville to search records? I rarely travelled into the city.

***

I presented the birth certificates to the clerk. "How come my parents aren't listed?"

The young woman examined them. "This one is the long form, the other the short. The short form doesn't list parents."

"Really? That's the only reason?"

"The short form is cheaper."

Stunned, I asked, "Could you look up my parents?"

"We can't give out that information." The clerk withdrew papers from a drawer. "You'll have to request the long form."

"I can't find out now?"

"We don't provide that information in person. You have to complete the forms and mail them back with the funds."

*****

Weeks passed before the anticipated document arrived. Heartbeats hurling to my throat increased the closer I neared the house from the mailbox. My very being depended upon answers in the envelope clutched in my hand—answers no one had seen fit to share. Perhaps either to delay or to savour, I sauntered as if the paper in my hand were a mere flyer and then, when the screen door slammed behind me, I debated where to sit before slitting the envelope. Perhaps I'd slit my wrists, too, when I was done.

I sat and opened the envelope. Blood rushed to my head. I read it a second time. I felt faint. I read it a third time.

Dad's words pounded at my ears. *"Ignore Aunty G… ignore her, ignore her, ignore her,"* and *"I told you your mother was your mother."*

The document slipped to the floor.

*****

I loathe Stonebrooke, and now I understand why Dad took Aunty G from here. My room is horrid. Food is horrid. Staff is horrid.

And the lumps never end—lumps in the mashed potatoes, lumps in the mattress, lumps in my body.

Dad, his voice strong and sure, haunts me. *"I told you Mom was your mother. Why wouldn't you believe me?"*

And I want to scream: *Why couldn't you have given me the truth.* No, he didn't lie, not technically. But he lied by omission, and aren't secrets just as bad as lies?

So what if Mom birthed me before Dad and she married? But why didn't Dad and Mom marry when she was pregnant with me? Why did he marry Augusta Jane Simmons? Did he cheat with Mom on Augusta? Did he even know Augusta when Mom became pregnant?

Obviously, Mom was his second choice or he would have married Mom first. Or could Mom have not told Dad about the pregnancy? Maybe she didn't want to force him into marriage. Was Augusta's death the catalyst for Mom and Dad to reunite, and if so, what prompted their reunion? Did Dad love one wife more than the other?

I sigh and wipe away tears. Despite having facts, I wish I had all the answers.

"Ignore Aunty G... ignore her..."

This story is fiction although there are two instances creatively written from facts. While researching my MacKenzies around 2000/2001, I conversed face to face with several elderly individuals in Kenzieville, Pictou County, Nova Scotia. From these conversations, I heard about a young man who several years previously was searching for his MacKenzies. His story was similar to that of fictional Isabelle's in that his great-grandmother Elizabeth had been sent to the United States to deliver her out-of-wedlock baby. With no one remembering the man's name, I was unable to locate him, but in 2015, he—Vincent—found me online. Vincent (my fourth cousin once removed) relayed the barrel story, which actually happened to his great-grandfather Ernest MacKenzie, the father of Elizabeth's baby. Ernest and his sister, Isobel, my second cousins twice removed, never married and remained together in the family home for many years. Coincidentally, Isobel had an out-of-wedlock child, too, and moved out west after she became pregnant, where she delivered her baby who was raised by her married sister.

REMEMBERING HALLEY
ART WHITE

This story is fiction, built on dozens of memories from a lifetime of meeting wonderful people and pursuing adventures like those portrayed here. Brier Island is very real and step-by-step familiar to Alice and me. We have ten grandsons, none of whom are twins. We have flown a Teflon kite from the hill above our farmstead, using a reel on a rod attached to a drill and one hundred feet of electric cord, to bring 'er home from great heights.

Although our twin grandkids were off-put by the pea soup ceiling, we relied on that old maxim "fog at seven, clear by eleven" not to spoil our annual Equinox/Birthday picnic. And it came to pass. The day was magnificent: azure skies, wispy clouds, facile breezes, and shirtsleeve warm despite it being the first day of fall.

Depending on the ferries, it was a ninety-minute drive to Brier Island, a promontory of Digby Neck, the wind-worn peninsula dividing Fundy and St. Mary's bays on Nova Scotia's western coast. Brier's a "must see" for rock hounds, birders, artists, and assorted lovers of seascapes, lighthouses, and fishing lore. Our family knows the island well.

This place was a picnic paradise: home of Joshua Slocum's cairn (In 1909, he soloed the globe in a twenty-one-foot sloop.), of rundown wharves and bait shacks from the depleted long-liner fishery, and of sundry surname descendants who host ferry loads of folks "from away" here to watch whales or hike the palisades, to photograph migratory birds or boil a lobster fresh from the crib.

Our birthday girl basked above us amid a deck of scrub spruce and wild aster. While at water's edge, our daughter's children and I searched rockweed-covered crags for green crabs, pink muscles, spiny urchins, periwinkles, and manifold tidal pool life.

As the ocean began to muscle its way higher, we playmates became mountain goats scurrying surefootedly upon car-size granite outcroppings, clinging perilously to their flanks with seasoned aplomb. We bounced smooth greenish stones ball-like across bouldered beaches: six, eight, sometimes ten bounces to a toss. Rachel was always pleased to out-bounce her brother; they were competitive in everything.

"Ahoy, matey, ship on the horizon!" one of us pirates would shout as a lobster boat plied along, hardly able to breach the wall of waves rolling west to east from Fundy to St. Mary's basin.

Soon, sun-bleached barnacles were submerged in the salty Atlantic, flagellating for microscopic meals before the tide withdrew to leave them high and dry again, twice a day since forever. Shell and fin fish preyed in the bubbly current among graceful grasses while we two-legged scavengers retreated to sandy terrain to hunt and pick through flotsam for drifted "treasures," a sure sign for Grandma to close her book and announce to the world: "Timme-fore-Lunnch..."

There was a lone government truck in the parking area when we turned into the well-groomed grounds of Western Light. The compound contained three Maritime-issue buildings (one the lightkeeper's quarters), a scattering of picnic tables anchored to the grass-and-granite knoll, and the light itself, a stocky, red-on-white obelisk whose refracting goblet beacon was barely visible in the late-noon sun.

The twins knew the drill. Each grabbed a handle on our wear-worn metal cooler and wrestled it to the table nearest the ocean, now resounding majestically below our line of sight. We oldsters shouldered the camera, binocs, our vintage thermos, and handmade pass-around towel, sewn on three sides to double as a litter sack.

"Ahoy, matey!" shouted the Randy atop the sturdy table deck. "Ship on the horizon..." They pointed to a campervan like our own, slowly navigating a tricky turn in the washboard access road.

"Looks like us," I said, "except for the dog." A golden lab leaned half its length out the passenger window, obscuring the person whose arm moored the beastie's backside.

"Mind if we let her run?" asked the driver rolling his window. "She's only part dog, mostly people—"

"Our kind of dog," I enjoined. "Let 'er rip!"

The couple, our age I guessed, smiled and said something to the lab before the door flew open, sending a golden arrow straightway to where our kids called, "Here, boy! Here, boy!" The lab leaped happily into the reckless embrace of these new young friends.

"Wish we had a video camera," yearned the driver. "Angie loves this! Angie's the dog..."

We learned the Coldwells were from Oregon, on the last leg of a summer-long road trip "seeing Canada stem to stern." Like us, Betty and Len were retired, campers with a VW Westphalia like ours, and had two grandchildren, dare I say it, like us. They loved Nova Scotia! "If we had started here," said Len, "we might not have gone anywhere else!"

"Join us for lunch, won't you?" induced my wife. "Angie's already found a home with the kids. We've plenty of food and would love to hear about your summer. It sounds grand."

"That would be nice," said Betty, "but we've got edibles that have to be eaten. Our fridge is on the blink. Tell you what, we'll toss 'em all together and call it a potluck."

"Sounds like church," said Len.

"Sounds like a winner," said I, "but let's call it a party: the first day of fall and Grandma's birthday!"

We had a grand time. The kids "discovered" peanut butter and banana on pumpernickel from Coldwell's larder, and we shared "Blueberry Grunt" from our dessert tray. Angie posted herself between the kids, gratefully accepting crusts, cookie crumbs, and several rounds of luncheon meat Betty deemed unsafe for human consumption.

We talked about trips, theirs and ours. We swapped retirement stories, mine five years ago, Len's a year later. Betty and Marge passed around pictures from their purses. Len and I compared mileage and tire wear of our nearly identical vehicles. It was like we'd always been friends...

The kids and Angie sat on the rocky ledge leading to the breakers and blue-green ocean. The tide had retreated and turned to swells. A seal cavorted in the kelp to the delight of our tablemates. A breeze kicked its heels in the lea of a shrouding sun.

"Well, Mother," said Len, "shall we fly 'er high today? Looks like ideal conditions."

"Let's do," said Betty, "and Len, maybe the children will help you?"

"My thoughts exactly." He winked, ambling to their van, from which he retrieved two bundles of shimmering material that looked like a recording studio after a tornado. "We named our daughter Halley after the comet that passed by on the twelfth of February, 1986. It was that or Valerie for Valentine's Day. Halley bought these for her children while still in utero," said Len. "The ones we never got to play with... on trips we never took."

We were pleased he felt free to continue.

"Halley's husband never knew he was going to be a father. An IED took out his Humvee. It was so hard for Halley—from deliriously in love, to shipwrecked, to depression, to a stay-in-bed pregnancy. We have an ultrasound print from her second trimester. I can't tell elbow from arm pit in the jumble, but their doctor had no trouble saying, 'The twins look just fine...' One of each, just like yours."

Betty touched Len's arm. "Long story short," she continued, "Halley drove her ten-speed into an open car door and fell into the path of a taxi. She and our grandkids died before help could arrive. We're still telling ourselves they're really gone."

Len added, "But we don't want them to be gone, so we fly the grandkids' kites for them. Silly, I know, but it's something we can do 'til we can come up with something else. The kites are very special, unlike any we've ever seen. May I show Randy and Rachel how to fly them?"

Marge clasped her hands and blinked to shut out tears. I managed to say, "They'd love it, I'm sure..."

And they did. They loved those huge pom-poms, stringing out yards and yards of Teflon tendrils behind those small diamond-shaped kites. Len was in his glory, showing Rachel how to cast off and coax the shimmering comet up, up, up to where she could hold the heavy-duty fishing rod on her own and reel away until one could only see a rust-coloured patch in the sky.

Typically, Randy said he knew how to do it and launched his kite with the greatest of ease, letting out spools of line to beat Rachel to the moon. It was fun. It was fun at a visceral level for all of us: oldsters and kids, kids present, kids at heart, kids remembered.

We exchanged cards and promises to keep in touch. The twins hugged Angie and the Coldwells as if they were their own. They hugged them in return, and us, of course.

Betty whispered in my ear, "This was a golden afternoon of memories. Thank you..."

Len looked me in the eye and said, "It was precious, my friend..."

The last week in October, FedEx delivered a package from Doug's Toys in Des Moines, Iowa. It was addressed to: **World's Grandest Parents**. Return address: **Halley's Mom and Dad.** Inside were four, premium-quality Teflon kites and four fifteen-hundred-foot spools of nylon line. The note attached said: "Randy, if you and Rachel tie your strings together, you just might be able to land on the moon."

FRAGMENTS FROM A FUTILE WAR
MAIDA FOLLINI

Between the eighteenth of June, 1812, when the United States declared war against Great Britain, and Christmas Eve, 1814, when the Treaty of Ghent was signed to end the war, Americans and British troops fought battles on land and sea. Off the coast of New England, Canadian and American privateers attacked each other's ports and shipping, while along the Canada/U.S. border, forts were captured and recaptured by one side or the other as warring parties fought over particular sites. One man who served along the Niagara Frontier during the War of 1812 was Ralph Howard, a young printer from Windsor, Vermont, who enlisted in the U.S. Army, leaving behind a wife and small son.

<u>May 30, 1814—Windsor, Vermont:</u>

Rhoda Howard heard the drum as she hurried around the corner from her house towards Hedge's Print Shop on the main street to bring Ralph his lunch. On the green in front of the church was a crowd of people following a uniformed man beating a drum. Beside him was an officer with two privates, one of them carrying an American flag. The other carried a banner on which was written "Defend Your Country" on one side and on the other, "Signing Bonus $15."

At the shop, Ralph and old Mr. Hedge, the owner, stood in the doorway, eyeing the procession which stopped near the bandstand, where the officer climbed up.

"Raid on Connecticut!" they all heard the officer announcing. "British Attack Pettipaug!"[2]

"Vermont may be attacked next!"

"Join the Army to defend your country!"

The crowd around the bandstand grew.

---

[2] A force of 136 British sailors & marines burnt 25 American privateering vessels in Pettipaug (now Essex), Connecticut, in April 1814

141

"Who's going to sign up first? Who is the brave hero who will defend Vermont? Who will be first to collect the signing bonus?"

A young man stepped forward. The crowd cheered. One of the soldiers took him aside to show him the enlistment paper he was to sign. Soon others joined him.

"Why, there's Caleb!" Ralph saw his friend, a six-foot-tall man in a checked wool shirt.

Rhoda said, "What will his father say?" Caleb farmed with his father and brothers on the rocky hills outside of Windsor.

"Come on, we've got work to do," old Hedge said and led the way back into the print shop.

"Here's your stew." Rhoda handed over the lunch pail to her husband. "It's hot. I have to go back." She had left one-year-old William in the care of her aunt. "Don't you go signing up."

But when he came home that evening, Ralph had fifteen dollars in his pocket and a copy of his enlistment paper in his hand, listing him as an artificer[3] in the U.S. Army.

"Your uncles fought in '75," he said, "and your Granddad was in the French War."

Rhoda frowned, tight-lipped. *What am I supposed to do? It's just me and the baby?* But she didn't say anything. Ralph took the fifteen dollars from his pocket and passed over ten dollars to her. "This'll help. I better keep five dollars for my trip. You get your aunt to stay with you. Or go live with my mother."

I will not! If things get bad, I'll go live with my mother!

Two days later, Rhoda walked with Ralph all the way to the edge of Windsor, where he was to meet his friend Caleb Webster, who also had joined the Vermont company.

Rhoda watched as her husband and Caleb joined the group of enlistees, who were shepherded by a uniformed sergeant leading them to camp. As the men took the road to New York State, their forms grew smaller and smaller until they turned a corner and were out of sight. Rhoda walked slowly home.

"He get off all right?" asked her aunt. Nodding, Rhoda took the baby from Aunt Hannah. The stove was hot. Auntie had cooked up soup for supper. The baby was noisy. Yet the scene in the kitchen seemed to fade, and instead, Rhoda saw her husband walking down the road to New York, getting smaller and smaller until he disappeared.

---

[3] artificer = a mechanic, probably based on his print-shop experience.

Why didn't I hug him before he left? She berated herself. She had been ashamed to, in front of all those other men.

July 4, 1814—Fort Erie, Upper Canada

Fort Erie, a British Fort opposite Buffalo on the Niagara River, passed back and forth between the British and the invading Americans during 1813 and 1814.

On the fourth of July, 1814, Ralph wrote in his small pocket diary: "Yesterday, we recaptured Fort Erie without a battle. The British had to surrender. No wonder! They had only one hundred fifty men and we were thirty-five hundred strong!"

The following days required the defending Americans to labour long and hard, strengthening the fortifications. Ralph, the mechanic, was charged with cleaning and repairing weaponry, straightening bayonets, and mending damaged flintlocks on the Springfield muskets.

"The British will come back," was the word amongst the troops. "And with a stronger force."

Fort Erie guarded the lake and was key to any advances by either side. Sure enough, in a few weeks, the Americans in the fort could see large troop movements of redcoats, just out of firing range. Surrounding the fort, the British settled in for a siege, sending cannon balls over to soften it up. Ralph and Caleb and the other troops stayed for the most part out of open spaces—like the parade ground in the middle of the fort. There was plenty of work to do in the tunnels inside the thick walls.

August 15, 1814—Fort Erie, Upper Canada

Someone pulled on Ralph's foot. "Get up, get up," Caleb woke him. "They're attacking!"

Unrolling from his blanket, Ralph felt in the dark for his boots and pulled them on. Inside the earthworks in the bunk room, the noise of the attack had been deadened, as if far away. But once out in the open, it became a mad squalling. From the ramparts, Ralph and Caleb could see mobs of redcoats trying to climb ladders up the fort's walls. Caleb rested his musket on the parapet beside Ralph's, both ready to fire on any enemy who made it up the wall.

But the Brits' ladders were too short! The attack seemed to be failing, until a look-out called, "They have breached the old bastion!"

Sure enough, the crumbling wall of the oldest part of the fort had been battered in, and hundreds of British were actually inside the walls, below the rampart where Ralph was stationed. Two thoughts chased each other across his mind. One, that his duty was to go down and fight the invaders; the other, that he and his companions would certainly be mobbed and killed by the hundreds of men below. Ralph readied his weapon. He must go. The dawn was coming—would this be his last day?

The sergeant rallied his company. Caleb and Ralph followed down the stone steps to repel the invaders, when an enormous explosion sounded from below. The old bastion heaved as if it would fly up to the sky. Earth pellets fell in Ralph's face. He raised his arm to protect himself, just before he was thrown against the wall by the blast.

"The magazine's exploded!" Caleb shouted.

The earthen-covered bastion settled down again, like a disturbed bed blanket, while the cries and screams of hundreds of attackers came up from underneath. The British bugles blew, the retreat was signalled, although few of those caught in the explosion were alive to respond. The attack had failed.

Ralph thought, *I will live another day.*

September 15, 1814—Fort Erie—2 a.m.

"Everyone have your tools?" the sergeant said, softly. Ralph and his companions nodded. He and Caleb looked at each other and grinned. Their faces were darkened with charcoal from the campfire, and only the sergeant carried a candle lantern, half-covered for this night attack. Each artificer carried a short-handled sledgehammer and a bundle of scrap iron. Caleb bumped into Ralph as they and the accompanying infantrymen slid out through the narrow-bent passageway in the rampart.

Trying to avoid dislodging gravel or making any noise, they slipped into the fosse and up the other side. Ralph crouched low, going through the underbrush between the fort and the besiegers. He came upon the first cannon before he expected it, hidden as it was by a heap of branches. A shout went up, as the British gun crews realized they were being attacked and soon in the dark, shots were fired, bayonets bloodied, and men pushed against each other in hand-to-hand fighting. Ralph went to his work, finding the cannon's touch hole, jamming a piece of iron into it and hammering it down.

As the mob swirled around him, he managed to get two artillery pieces disabled before a huge British soldier grabbed him. "None of that, now." The Brit stuck his bayonet towards Ralph's throat. "Drop it."

Ralph dropped his hammer and put his hands over his head. As he was pushed and pulled by his captor towards the British camp, he stepped on a man's hand. It was Caleb, who was on the ground clutching his chest.

"Ralph! Help!"

Ralph's captor growled, "We'll take him, too!" pulling Caleb up by the shoulder. "Come on! We've got you now."

How they got to the British camp, Ralph scarcely knew, the Brits' bayonet poking into his back, while Caleb, bleeding heavily, stumbled as his arm was held fast in the captor's grip. Behind them, they could see their fort lit by the rising sun—out of reach. As they were led into captivity, they were unaware that the sortie they and their companions had made had broken the British siege. With cannons disabled and hundreds of men killed, the British withdrew in a few days.

September, 1814—On the road to Quebec

One foot in front of another, then another, and another. The long column of American prisoners straggled along the road, some of them with bandaged arms or legs; others, like Ralph, untouched, but dirty, tired, and with unkempt uniforms. Caleb, with his bayonet wound bandaged, was among the severely injured in a cart.

"How far are we walking?" one prisoner asked.

"You'll find out when we get to Quebec," the guard answered.

Quebec! That was hundreds of miles! After several days of walking with minimal food—some soup and bread handed around at the end of the day—Ralph's boots hurt him. The nails poked up into his feet. He stuffed some leaves and grass in his boots, but it didn't help much.

Progress was slow. Many prisoners were in bad shape, and the guards had a hard time keeping the column together. Ralph tried to think if being a prisoner was better or worse than a fighting soldier. It was better, he supposed, in that no one was shooting at them. But worse in the fact that the food was scarce and terrible, and the British guards weren't gentle in kicking the prisoners to ensure orders were obeyed.

Without comment, Ralph took his turn pulling the cart with wounded prisoners. His cart carried his friend Caleb and three others, one a man from Vermont but from Barrington, not Windsor, and two from Connecticut. Caleb's wound had been bandaged by a British surgeon so he wasn't bleeding, but every time the cart went over a bump, he groaned. At night, when the column stopped, Ralph tried to get him to eat by feeding him soup with a spoon. Caleb could only take a few spoonfuls at a time. "Do you think we'll make it back?" Caleb asked him. "I don't want to die up here."

"Some say we might be exchanged." Ralph tried to sound hopeful. But he knew it was mostly the officers who were exchanged.

All through the last of September and into October, the column of prisoners made its way along the north shore of the St. Lawrence River, through forests, past farms and villages, stopping at night to build cooking fires and have their meagre suppers, sleeping often in barns commandeered by the British officers but sometimes under the open sky, huddled under blankets around a fire to keep warm. Ralph stayed by Caleb, making sure the guards poured the ration of soup or stew into Caleb's tin pot as well as his own. But Caleb grew weaker.

One evening, Caleb said, "I don't know any prayers. I was mostly out huntin' on a Sunday. Do you know any prayers?"

Ralph nodded. Hadn't he been to church every Sunday for twenty years, until he went in the Army?

"Say one for me," said Caleb.

Ralph began mumbling out the "Our Father..." but seeing the feverish look in Caleb's eyes, he spoke out straight and serious, and Caleb joined him in the amen and gave a sigh of relief. The lights from the campfires flickered, muffled voices of the men around them faded away as the prisoners went to sleep. Only the guards taking duty remained awake, walking their beats. When Ralph woke the next morning and unrolled from his blankets, Caleb was cold and still.

Ralph felt somber. There was no time to grieve—he had to get up, eat his morning ration, and be ready to march when the British guards gave the order. As he rolled up his blankets, Ralph thought, *I'll miss having someone from home to talk to. I'll miss taking care of him and trying to feed him up.*

The men around them were still asleep. The guard was at the end of his beat, talking with another Britisher. Ralph looked at Caleb's pale face, his clothes disarrayed from tossing in pain during the night, his legs extended in death, his boots... They were good boots, strong cowhide, laced up around his calves, scuffed but without any obvious holes in them. Ralph glanced towards the guards. They were still murmuring to each other.

Quickly, Ralph unlaced Caleb's boots, pulled them off—trying to be careful although he knew Caleb was beyond feeling anything. He crouched down behind the knapsacks and bedrolls. Kicking off his own boots, Ralph pulled on Caleb's—they fit well, slightly larger than his own, but no nails had worked through to cut into his sore feet. God, what a relief! Ralph took his old worn-out boots, loosening the laces, and pulled them on Caleb's stiffened feet. Then he moved away, took his bedroll over near another sleeping prisoner, and pretended to be asleep.

"Another for the dead cart!" shouted the guard to his mate, when he checked on the Yankee prisoner who failed to wake when the reveille was sounded.

November 18, 1814—Quebec

In Quebec, the exhausted prisoners were crowded onto ships. Ralph tried to settle on deck as much as possible where the air was better, but the prisoners had to muster twice a day to be counted. They had to serve their turns, emptying the sanitary pots and cleaning the decks. By the time the vessel reached Halifax, Ralph felt as dirty as if he had been crawling in mud and scratch as much as he would, he couldn't stop the itch from flea bites.

December, 5, 1814—Melville Island, Halifax

At least we are off the ship. The three tiers of bunks in the prison camp stayed still and didn't roll back and forth. The food was revolting slops, and Ralph scarcely wanted to eat it. His energy and his appetite were gone. At night, he sat with the other prisoners around the fire and tried to join in as they sang songs to keep their spirits up.

But he kept wondering what was happening back home. Little William would be walking and talking now. *I wonder how Rhoda is managing.* Ralph could hardly remember how it felt to hold her and see her smile. Windsor was like a dream village, shingled houses and white-painted church like something seen in a picture book. He often thought of the print shop with its presses, and old Hedge peering at his work and checking it, pointing out his mistakes. Sometimes he reminded himself of the way the letters were set out in the cases—

moving his hands in the air to set up a sentence of type as if he were completing an order.

Why had he ever enlisted? He couldn't remember now the feelings of patriotism he had held. He hadn't wanted to be left behind when the neighbourhood young men had joined as a company and gone with their own elected officer to join the army. It seemed far away as if it had happened to a different person.

He missed Caleb, and whenever he looked at his boots, he felt a twinge of guilt that he had taken them off his dead friend's feet. He attached himself to other New England men, anyone from Vermont or New Hampshire, to remind him of home. They would talk about their farms, their work, their families. To fill the empty hours, Ralph gathered small pieces of driftwood from the shore and carved them into miniature farm animals: a cow and calf, a horse's head, a sheep dog. Once, for a joke, he carved a miniature pig and gave it the name of a guard they all hated; then they burned it in the cooking fire. Grinning and spouting insults about the guard gave a few moments of satisfaction.

January, 1815—Melville Island, Halifax

It wasn't fair. His body had turned enemy on him. The runs forced him to go to the latrine repeatedly. An officer of the guard said he would have to move to the hospital part of the prison. The bed was better—low near the floor rather than the highest one of a tier of three. Ralph had stopped thinking of the British guards as "the enemy." Some even tried to help him. They brought him and the other patients soup instead of the hard bread and tough beef served to the other prisoners. After a while, it was too much effort to get out of bed. Sometimes another prisoner would be detailed to clean him up.

An officer brought in a chaplain.

"Do you have anything you want to say?" the chaplain said. Ralph shook his head.

"Then say a prayer with me. Do you know the Lord's Prayer?"

As he muttered "Our Father who art in Heaven" with the chaplain, Ralph thought of the time he had said the prayer for Caleb. Now he was saying it for himself.

Then he said, "Reverend, I worry about my wife, Rhoda. I want to say I'm sorry. I said I would come home and I haven't."

The chaplain gave him a rueful smile. "We all have our regrets," he said. Then he went on to the soldier in the next bed.

January 11, 1815—Deadman's Island, Halifax

"**H**ere's another load," said the guard. They placed six corpses in the lighter, and the oarsmen rowed them over to Deadman's Island. More recent prisoners, who were still in a strong condition, had extended the burial hole for the mass grave. One by one, the bodies, wrapped in canvas, were placed in the pit. The chaplain and an officer each said a prayer. Then the prisoners shovelled earth over their former comrades.

March, 1815—Windsor, Vermont

A man knocked on Rhoda Howard's door. William, age almost two, ran to the door and pulled the latch to open it. Rhoda got up from the rocking chair where she had been holding the sleeping one-month-old baby. As she recognized one of the Vermont company who had left the previous summer, Rhoda's heart gave a leap—perhaps Ralph was coming home? At the same time, she felt a clutch of dread. "Do you have any news?" she asked. "Have you seen Ralph?"

The man looked away, awkwardly. "I'm sorry," he said. "It was in a prison camp. He died of illness. It wasn't as if he were shot or wounded. They had a hospital at the camp. A lot of men died."

Rhoda couldn't look at him. She had known, for a long time, that Ralph might not come back. For an instant, she had hoped the soldier at the door would give her good news. But no—it was as she feared. Ralph would never know about the new baby who was named after him. Her two boys' father would never come home. Ralph would never get up in the morning to go to work in the print shop. Never come home at night, to hold her. It was over.

Ralph Howard was captured at Fort Erie on September 17, 1814, and died January 10, 1815. He was one of 195 American prisoners who died at the Melville Island military prison in Halifax. Most were buried in mass graves on nearby Deadman's Island.

The war ended with the Treaty of Ghent, on the twenty-fourth of December, 1814. However, news of the Treaty did not reach Halifax until March 1815—too late for Ralph.

Memorial Day Ceremony on Deadman's Island,
May 29, 2005

JOURNEY'S END
ART WHITE

This story, liberally sprinkled with author's license, is essentially factual, in as much as five decades of memory can be trusted. It was my father's gift to us kids.

My father was forty-five when I was born. I was thirty-one when he died, the same age he was when his father died. Grandfather White painfully succumbed to black lung disease after years of retching up sputum and never drawing a satisfactory breath. My father died in his sleep on the porch of a summer cottage overlooking a familiar seascape, where our family had vacationed every summer since before the war, when gas rationing meant our journey to Tenants Harbor, Maine, was by train.

Dad made reservations the previous summer with the daughter of the curmudgeonly sea captain he had dealt with for years: four oceanside cottages, off the narrow road from Thomaston to the ferry landing at Port Clyde.

Predictably, Catherine Martin would have asked my father the previous summer, "Will you be wantin' the same two weeks again next year, Mr. White?"

"Last full week of July, first of August," would have been his reply. "We've found that's best. May I give you a deposit now?"

"That won't be necessary, Mr. White, but I'll need half the rental by the first of June, if you please."

They both knew the routine. Next, she'd say, "It's hard to find renters once the season's started, don't ya know." He'd offer to write her a cheque for the full amount. She'd feign surprise, but accept the remittance, insisting on "no increase in price, if you're taking the four [cottages]..."

That was how negotiations had gone since our family started vacationing on this stretch of rockbound coast in the early thirties.

The summer of our last reunion, two dozen of us congregated in the four cottages. Bill's family shoe-horned into a squat one-bedroom dwelling on the sloping hillside behind a trio of two-storey, side-by-side summer houses perched in the sand twenty or so feet from the high waterline of dried seaweed, assorted flotsam, and silvered driftwood.

The "Shanty" was an off-square weatherboard building, painted a hue my artist brother called "aqua-bilge." He and Rose started out in the tiny windowless bedroom with the brass four-poster. Their daughters shared the foldout chesterfield; Mike slept on a foam slab under the tubular table in the kitchen. The sag and creak of that vintage bed soon convinced them to offer the girls a "room of their own," forgoing a bit of privacy for a good night's sleep.

John and Grace's larger family drew the far cottage, a faux Cape Cod bungalow with sun-bleached cedar shingles. "It's the only one with maritime character," boasted John who, like Bill, was a serious avocational sculptor. Cousins of all ages also appreciated its playhouse charm and congregated there most days, much to the carvers' chagrin (and our approbation).

Apparently first built, the big house came equipped with a vine-covered, crescent-in-the-door, two-hole privy that made relieving oneself a city kid's adventure. It also had the largest fireplace (the cottage, not the privy), a horseshoe pit with rebar stakes and locally-made shoes, *and* a peeled-spruce boat-slip, replete with a home-made, blunt-nosed, flat-bottomed rowboat made by Captain Martin himself.

The "shapers of wood" set up a whittling area at the headway "to keep an eye on the kids," they claimed. In truth, no child could launch that hefty skiff nor suffer any more than shivers in that frigid, shallow, rocks-for-a-beach, briny cove (no wonder we never met a fisherman who could swim!).

Dottie's family of six, plus Dad and my sister Polly, overflowed the middle cottage. Actually, things were quite cozy. Dad, who snored, slept solo on the screened porch; Polly, who also snored, took up a tiny, windowless backroom. The rest settled anywhere there was space to stretch out, mostly on cots or inflatable mattresses. During the day, the children went next door to play horseshoes, hide-and-seek around the privy, or piece together a jigsaw puzzle (one was always on the go). Adults (sans the wood shapers) were likely to hold sway in Dottie's big kitchen, planning the day or just catching up on the year since we last got together.

My family arrived in the night, at a wee hour, on Sunday morning, headlights poking bright shafts of light up and down, as our fully packed van negotiated the bumpy road to the beach. We'd driven straight through from Cincinnati and should have been eyelid heavy, but everyone was wide awake.

"Smell the ocean!" piped up my wife, Alice.

"I smell the mouldy ice house!" said Brad, our firstborn, whose head was perched on the backrest between us. "When *Dad* was a boy," he gruffed in his deepest voice, "he had to carry a BIG block of ice to each of the cottages."

"And he had to do it Every-Day-But-Sunday!" chimed in Mark, our preschooler, punctuated by our daughter Chris' infectious giggle.

The smells were distinctive and delicious: slightly sulphurous ocean air mixed with a dash of fir and spruce. Rounding down into the compound, the olfactory greeting completed itself with a hint of birch smoke coming from the near cottage, the one whose porch was lit. Our cottage. We had arrived.

"They're here! They're here!" squealed Polly, waving without looking as she stepped cautiously off the porch. My father remained at the door, framed in the welcoming backlight of the wood-panelled main room.

"Dad said you'd be here by two! You must be dead tired after all that driving. And here's little Mark," doted the kids' favourite aunt. "Chris and Brad, what puffy eyes you have! It's so-o-o good to see you all again. This is your cottage, Art, same as last year. Dad built a fire to take off the chill. I made the beds, same old beds. Oh, here are the dogs! Such good dogs. You must be tired. Everyone's here, even Nancy with her leg in a cast. Oh, this is going to be our best summer ever!"

Chris and Brad took a flashlight to walk the dogs. Mark went with Polly to see where he'd sleep. We left the van packed, greeted my tired-looking father, said good night, quick-toured the familiar bungalow, turned back the slightly musty quilts, tucked in the kids and then ourselves, and slept like logs until the dogs announced a bevy of cousins and aunts, all led (and out-sung) by my father in a vainglorious chorus of "Oh what a bu-tee-full morrr-ning..."

The day started in Dottie's kitchen with fresh blueberry pancakes slathered in local maple syrup, and things got better from there. Brothers and sisters, uncles, aunts, and cousins walked and talked and played together with a comfort and presumption belying the year we'd been apart.

Especially memorable were the private moments my father convened with each of us. He and Alice chatted around the kitchen: he washed, she dried; he filleted and floured a flounder, she fried it up and fixed the veggies.

After lunch, I launched the rowboat on its maiden voyage and then sat with Alice in matching Adirondack chairs to watch the foursome: Dad at the helm, Brad rowing, kids pouring out stories, Grandpa asking the right questions, listening, enjoying. I saw him raise his shirt to show off the outline of his new pacemaker buried within the muscle-wall of his skinny, concave chest. He did his ogre shtick: pocketing his glasses, mussing his hair, removing his upper plate, leaving a single tobacco-stained tooth that guarded an expansive aperture of flaccid lips and sunken cheeks. Ugly! Our kids loved it, as always.

Dad and I sat together before supper, just the two of us, legs dangling off a picnic table. Our conversation touched on Alice and the kids, on my work and his retirement years, on his plans and my plans, on wide-ranging reminiscences and deep-seated satisfactions. It was good. Very good.

Dad ate supper at his cottage. I don't remember what we did. We may have made fireplace popcorn in the long-handled popper. I know we bedded down early, feeling the full-faced tiredness of a day on the road and not enough rest due to that sow-bellied mattress.

Alice and I woke with the sun, left a fridge note for the kids, and took the dogs to the beach. Overnight, a spring tide had left extra goodies for the dogs to prospect, and prospect they did, rolling in every kelp cluster, nosing every sea-borne carcass and jellyfish puddle.

Dottie met us as we turned for home.

"Looks like you just got up," I quipped, prompted by my sister's doleful look. Dottie's hands crossed just below her chin as she said softly, "Dad died in his sleep. I found him ten minutes ago."

Dad-died-in-his-sleep…

Upon reflection, we all agreed our father had "called the shot" on the last chapter of his bountiful life, the last chapter and more. I say he got to write his very own ending, down to the obit: *W.L. White died in his sleep.*

Dottie said Beth had been tip-toe-attentive retrieving her colouring book from the wicker table in the corner next to where her grandpa lay sleeping. She didn't see the crayon can atop its open pages. It crashed like a cymbal against the wooden deck. Dottie heard and came to investigate. Dad would have liked the poignant irony.

We cried when we told our kids at breakfast.

Later, the five of us gathered at his bedside. His stubbled cheeks were stiff and cool against my kiss; his thin hand was alabaster beneath our children's wary pats. Dad was so still.

I don't remember who drove to the highway to make the phone calls. I don't remember who took the children to the beach. I don't remember the doctor arriving or examining or saying anything except, "I'll call the funeral home for you—there's only one."

We stood on the porch watching the elderly physician's cherry-red sports car bob and weave along the birch-lined lane until the sound of calm waves lapped louder than the distant growl of horsepower.

"Now what do we do?" asked Bill after we gathered in the middle house. "What comes next?"

I suggested we direct the mortician to have the body transported to New Jersey and buried alongside our mother, brother Robert, and sister Nancy, and that we opt for the minimum mortuarial requirement. Nothing fancy: just embalming and some kind of container shipped by common carrier. We would ask George Talbott, Dad's life-long pastor and friend, to preside at a memorial in twelve days' time after we finished the two weeks pre-arranged for our enjoyment (and now, for our shared grief).

After some discussion, we agreed on *minimum requirement.* Dad would have approved.

I relayed our wishes to the funeral director, an overly-dressed, portly gent who smelled of flowers and had an annoying habit of trying to end my sentences before I was ready.

He said, "It would be cheaper to drive to New Jersey since the closest airport or train is Portland." He confirmed that interstate law required embalming that, he stressed, was "included in the price of the casket." From the laminated pages of a pass-around binder, he recommended a tasteful model, "our most popular," he told us, nodding as if the deal were already closed.

I asked, "How much it would be with only the *necessary* professional services?"

He hesitated. "Let's call it $900. Of course, that wouldn't include roundtrip mileage to New Jersey or per diem and overnight accommodations for the driver."

I pushed further. "This is your *least* expensive coffin? Only professionals will see it."

Taken aback, he looked around the table, appealing, as it were, to my siblings. "Well, there's always the *welfare* box," he said with funereal intonation, knowing full well we were too close to death to remain practical, much less as frugal as our Depression-tested father. We took the $900 package.

Earlier, all the children had watched the shrouded body wheeled to the hearse. A few tarried, peering every now and again through the parted velvet curtains or touching his white wool blanket airing on the line between the cottages.

In the aftermath of all that transpired, our family of five decided to hike the shoreline. There on a wave-splashed granite perch, our preschooler asked for the first of many times, "Is Grandpa still alive?"

I looked at Alice and she at me. "Grandpa's dead, Mark. Remember how cold he felt? Your grandfather died in his sleep, in the bed where we saw him this morning. The man with the long black car will put Grandpa in a wooden box and bury him in the ground near his house in New Jersey, like we did with Lucky in our backyard. Remember? We'll go and see his grave after we finish our vacation."

Touching his chest and looking perplexed, he said, "But Grandpa's alive. He told us the little machine would keep his heart going for a long time to come. The battery lasts for *two* years."

Alice and I exchanged moist-eyed looks. We both remembered the picture: my bare-chested, skinny father out in the rowboat with our three kids, with *this* trusting, impressionable little kid. Dad told such vivid stories. Clearly, he had saved his best for last.

"See where they cut me open?" he must have said, with a serious look and urgent tone. "Here, you can feel the little machine that will keep my heart going for a long time to come. Right here, feel it? It's got a tiny battery that tells my heart, *'keep going, keep going, keep going.'* A tiny battery that lasts for two years. Here, feel it. Feel it? Right here..."

Again and again that day, that week, that month, Mark continued to believe. "Is Grandpa still alive?" Lying on his back by the fireplace, guiding the shopping cart around a local market, from the backseat of the van on our way to New Jersey: "Is Grandpa still alive?" Mark assured us over and over again, "The battery lasts for *two* years."

EXPIRED OPTION
ELIZABETH MCGINLEY

Trading in financial derivatives was instrumental to the collapse of global markets in 2008 to 2009, resulting in the Great Recession. Contrary to popular belief, wealth wasn't lost; it was transferred from the economically challenged to the rich. In the end, death is the great equalizer. Is it possible for that wealth to find its way back into the pockets of those from whom it was taken?

It was a warm day in early autumn when he received the news. No one called or came to deliver it in person. The tired postman who stood patiently at the front door while he signed for the registered letter was the sole human present at that fateful moment. Even he wasn't aware of the life-changing significance he held in his hand. The news was delivered without sympathy or remorse.

Thaddeus Bartholomew Dunvegin threw the envelope on the table and looked out at the mirror that was the Bay of Fundy. The air was so still and the water so calm that life itself held its breath in anticipation of what he would do with the news. The forest of trees across the bay was ablaze with fall colours, and their reflection in that mirror intensified the brilliance seized by a painter who had tossed his palette in frenzied ecstasy. Only the passion of a master to create something that would capture his joy could have rendered that scene. Until today, Thaddeus had never realized how intimate and alive that view was from his window.

He turned off the television that had been mute all morning. The S&P 500 was forty points higher at nineteen ninety-eight, and with mere hours to go until the bell rang, it was unlikely to close below the nineteen fifty level. He made his entry on the spreadsheet. The nineteen fifty puts he had written would expire worthless.

He took a deep breath, paused briefly, and tore the letter open. The typed words ran cold and impersonal across the page. The replica signature of some medical official testified that no human hand had pressed a pen to that paper.

Someone must have stuffed the registered envelope, but did that person read what they sent? Impersonal, detached, medicinal, yet ominous: *Bone cancer test: POSITIVE. An oncologist will contact you within the next five days.*

What could doctors and their dubious medicine do for him now? He had read about bone cancer, the treatments that were used, and the odds of being cured. It all pointed to months of appointments with specialists, follow-up visits with more specialists, and in the end, dying anyway. Along the way to dying, he would be greeted with sympathy and mock sadness from people who didn't know or really care about him. His pride couldn't tolerate the scene laid out for him. Why not put that valuable time to better use? He deserved to savour every priceless moment allotted to him.

He gazed out the window again, anxious to remove his eyes from the offensive piece of paper. To look at the painting rendered by that unseen hand outside, marvel at the strangeness of the monkey-puzzle tree in the yard, study the collection of Rosenthal plates in the cabinet—to cast his eyes anywhere except on that cold, callous page. It wasn't a letter. To give it that name implied writing, correspondence, a hand flying across the page to capture thought. No, this was a summons that Thaddeus Bartholomew Dunvegin wouldn't obey.

He put on his light overcoat and walking shoes, locked the door, and strolled to the office of his old friend and solicitor in Wolfville. There was no time like the present to get his affairs in order.

***

He had to wait fifteen minutes to see Alastair. The passage of time was more frenetic now, not the slow-motion decay that happened weekly with the option writing. With that activity, each day saw the erosion of the option values and the increase of his net worth. The pattern had suddenly reversed this morning. Time and Thaddeus were now sworn enemies.

"Dunny. What a pleasant surprise. I was just about to grab a late lunch."

"Coffee will do," replied Thaddeus.

"Is this business we can discuss outside? I need to get out of the office."

Knowing how Thaddeus hated offices, Alastair's offer was received with the predictable pleasure of his friend.

They settled into the comfortable lounging chairs at Thaddeus' favourite coffeehouse. Students went there to write or perspire over a stack of books in preparation for examinations. The atmosphere breathed work filled with life, something Thaddeus secretly craved in his solitary occupation.

"How's business?" Alastair's innocent question was so removed from what occupied Thaddeus' mind that he loathed answering it.

"Profitable," he replied sarcastically.

"I wish you'd manage my money," prompted Alastair. "Remind me, how do you make twenty percent a year, regardless of what the market does?"

Thaddeus smiled. "Time decay. I write options on the S&P 500 and let them expire worthless. And the returns are closer to twelve percent."

"Too esoteric for me," sighed Alastair before biting into his chicken salad sandwich.

"For every buyer of options, there must be a seller. Since eighty percent of all options expire worthless, it's the seller who usually profits." Thaddeus made the statement mechanically as though responding to an oral test.

"I guess the trick is not to sell the twenty percent that have value."

"To write," corrected Thaddeus. "The proper term is to write— think of insurance underwriters."

"Who buys these options?" asked Alastair.

"On the S&P 500? Not your granny or the old widow down the street. That's why I do it. My conscience never bothers me when I'm taking from the banks and the idle rich." Thaddeus brushed a hand through his salt and pepper hair. "But I didn't come here to talk about options, not that kind anyway."

"Are you looking for legal counsel? Trouble with the bank?" Alastair grinned.

"No, I need a will."

"A will?" The remains of Alastair's sandwich hung precariously between his thumb and forefinger.

"Last Will and Testament, you do know what that is?" Thaddeus answered.

"Of course, but you've always avoided drafting one—at my perpetual prodding, I might add—because it's morbid."

"The hoard's compounded nicely over the past five years, and I've got to think about what to do with it if I—" He broke off, not wanting to use the dreaded word that would finish both himself and the sentence.

Alastair scrutinized him. The mass of black hair tinged with grey circled his well-formed face. The large brown eyes, always with a tinge of melancholy, blended with his aquiline nose. His tall, thin frame was regal and straight. Thaddeus exuded that rare confidence possessed by a man who knew his own mind. And yet there was an unsettled quality about him as though he were being hunted. Alastair envied his freedom from family obligations, but not to the extent that he wanted to wear his shoes.

"I've never understood you, Dunny. You're a handsome man, intelligent, caring and rich—let's not forget rich. Why didn't you marry?"

Without thinking, Thaddeus answered, and for the first time in his life, it was the most honest answer he had given to that question.

"I never wanted to, period. Have I regretted it? No. Have I ever loved? Yes. Did I love enough to spend my *entire* life with one person? No. Unless death takes both of you at precisely the same moment, you'll die alone anyway. Enough said."

"Not if you're the one who goes first. Who gets the hoard?"

"That's where I need your help. And don't waste any time. Make it a priority for a friend."

"What's the rush?"

"Nothing." Thaddeus thought for a moment. "It's on the irritating, long-standing *to-do* list, and I want to scratch it off."

"Manage my money, and I'll waive the fee," suggested Alastair.

"Money mixed with friendship yields a dish most foul," he replied.

Thaddeus knew he could count on Alastair and the greed of bankers to find a suitable home for the hoard.

In the weeks that followed, Alastair put him in touch with a foundation operated by a major bank that allowed Thaddeus to establish his own trust. He could direct the funds as his heart desired. He negotiated back and forth with increasing impatience about the terms and wording of the trust. The funds were to be allocated to gifted, underprivileged children who showed aptitude in any field except finance and technology. He was adamant that the world didn't need another banker or computer programmer. After expending considerable energy drafting and re-drafting the terms of the trust, he finally got exactly what he wanted.

But Thaddeus craved something more, something personal, something he could put his hands on now. He wanted to sow seeds and see some life begin to grow before he became another dead philanthropist. He *needed* to find a child to be the recipient of at least a part of that vast fortune. But where in the world should he start his search?

***

The flight over the Atlantic turned Thaddeus' concentration to his travels over the past few years. During that time, he hadn't once visited the country of his father's birth. He had quit his job with an engineering firm in Montreal five years ago and settled down to a quiet life in the Annapolis Valley. He had endured ups and downs with the options trading over those years but always managed to come out ahead. He used his money to travel, see the world, and try to forge a connection with mankind. He journeyed to the Himalayas, Egypt, Kenya, Peru, but deliberately avoided Scotland after burying his mother in the family plot six years ago. The country had held nothing for him, just the buried remains of those he had most cherished. The magnificent landscape and his idyllic childhood memories were overshadowed by funerals—one after the other—for his father's parents, his closest aunt, and finally his own mother and father. With these last two gone and no siblings, no offspring, and only cousins and distant relatives on his father's side scattered across the globe, Thaddeus felt quite alone in the world. The geographical challenges of that brood left him with nothing more than pictures taken decades ago, now hidden between the pages of dusty family albums.

For the past six months after the short, sharp pains started and apprehension about the time he had left preoccupied his mind, he felt the presence of some *other* in his midst. It was in his house, beside him on his walks, sitting across from him at the table, and he couldn't get it to leave. He wondered if this *other* wanted him to track down his relations and leave any survivors a healthy bequest. Prudence and common sense put an end to that whim. From his father, he learned that most of these people were comfortable, the children well educated, while others were in business or working in golden handcuff jobs for various governments. When the guilt of legacy seized him, Thaddeus envisioned a rush of strangers, united merely by the Dunvegin name, queuing up to claim their share of the much-coveted hoard. No, that would never do. His father would have cursed him from his seat next to the Great Almighty for bestowing financial generosity on any of them.

"We all came from the same stock, and we all made our way in the world. We owe each other nothing."

His father's standard line about family legacies was in direct opposition to his nature. A kind and generous man, James Dunvegin had been utterly devoted to his small family. He worked all the hours God sent from the time he was twelve years old. His formal schooling was interrupted at sixteen when he took *the Queen's shilling*. He had added two years to his age when questioned by the official, a small lie that was easily believed given his strong build and mature face. He joined the British army and headed to Egypt. The Suez Crisis was in full swing, and James distinguished himself by learning Arabic and strengthening Britain's local ties with the natives. He eventually emigrated, settling in Montreal and marrying a local girl.

His wanderlust continued with various postings at what was then known as the Department of External Affairs. Five years after retirement, he died of a brain haemorrhage, saving the Canadian government a considerable sum in indexed pension payments for what should have been at least another twenty-five years.

Thaddeus' mother was a gentle soul with a passion for Conan Doyle. It was to this unfortunate obsession with all things Sherlock Holmes that he owed his accursed name. He loved his mother but never forgave her for christening him with a name that didn't even lend itself to acceptable aliases. Moreover, he felt that anyone with the surname Dunvegin should never call their child Thaddeus Bartholomew. He had lived his entire life being called Dunny—the logical nickname to be extracted from the three pompous choices he was forced to wear like a bad joke on his identity cards.

In the Scottish vernacular, even Dunny was humiliating. It meant "basement" or "dungeon." The irony of its association with six feet under wasn't lost on him. Thaddeus smiled at Fate's cruel humour.

"You can choose your friends, but you can't choose your relatives." His father's sage expression repeated itself to him as the plane soared along. Thaddeus believed that to be true of children. Suppose he had been the father of one or more tiresome brats? He had friends who were loath to talk about what their adult children were up to because it didn't amount to very much. Children were wonderful until they reached their early teens as Thaddeus had discovered when he tutored grade-school children in math and English. They were delightful companions: honest, straightforward, and constantly curious about the world. When they turned thirteen, they morphed into self-centred creatures that couldn't wait to insult the adults they so fervently wanted to become. Why couldn't childhood last forever?

As his father had said about relatives, Thaddeus preferred to choose his child.

***

Thaddeus dropped his bags at the hotel and made his way through Glasgow Central. The overnight flight had not yielded rest, preoccupied as he was with the search for a child and memories of his family. Despite his illness—or to spite it—he felt full of energy and resolve.

He loitered around the old train station. The hum and buzz of people rushing to and from the platforms filled him with excitement.

A woman's voice echoed throughout the station as she called out familiar places in a clear Glaswegian accent. "The 10:50 train with service to Paisley, calling at Pollockshaws, Crossmyloof, and Barrhead is leaving from Platform Four."

Almost immediately, there was another broadcast and the rush was on. The minute hand of the clock hanging in the centre of the station moved slowly toward the appointed time of the next train. Thaddeus watched with fascination and contempt as time slipped by. What price would he pay to turn those eager hands back to the halcyon days of his childhood?

He had looked up at that clock as a boy, holding tight to his father's hand while they listened for the next train to Edinburgh. The station was shabbier in those days, and it was a man's gruff voice that rang out over the loudspeaker, but the tense atmosphere and twin aromas of pastry and panic hadn't altered.

It was mid-December then, too, and his mother had wanted to do some Christmas shopping before taking in a play in Edinburgh. Thaddeus had been looking forward to spending Christmas with his paternal grandparents. All three of them had made their way from London where his father had been posted for five years, dressed in warm clothes and holding tight to each other in the bustle of Euston station. His parents' warmth mingled with the smell of hot gingerbread and chestnuts—protection, security, love—they were happy days.

The soft glow of white lights decorating the station filled his childhood heart with anticipation, not for the presents that Father Christmas would bring but for the presence of his parents, grandparents, aunties, and uncles filling the house on Christmas morning. Was this a memory of his life, or was it a scene from someone else's in a book he'd read long ago?

An unseen hand grazed his shoulder. He turned, but no one was there. The hand propelled him out of the station, into a florist's shop, and then into a taxi. He told the driver to take him to the Necropolis Cemetery in Glasgow's east end. He didn't want to go there yet. He wanted to soak up the city atmosphere and live a little.

Why had he given the driver that location? The *other* was once again seated beside him, but no one was there. Thaddeus rolled down the window, threw his head out, and breathed in the brisk, fresh morning air. He hummed a tune, but the presence didn't leave as the streets passed by in slow motion.

Grudgingly, he resigned himself to this *other*, accepted it, and finally welcomed it like an old friend.

***

Time decay. The phrase repeated in his head. The word *decay* became ominous to him now as he stood among the gravestones that stretched in a long queue before him. Somewhere in this cemetery, his mother's ashes were buried beside those of his father, to rest for all eternity in this foreboding place.

The office of the caretaker was closed, so he had to work from memory to find his parents' plot and that of his father's family. He checked his watch; it was after one. Where had the time gone? It was just ten o'clock when he stood in Glasgow Central. The unseen hand had stolen those three precious hours.

He meandered from one tombstone to the next. There were hundreds of them, and he wondered how long it would take to find the ones that connected him to the Necropolis.

He passed Thomas Lipton. The once-famous tea merchant and yachtsman had bought the three Glasgow tearooms of Thaddeus' grandfather. Tommy had never married and had no children; his vast fortune had been bequeathed to the City of Glasgow. Did anyone remember Lipton? After all his travels, he chose the Necropolis in the neighbourhood of his youth as his final resting place. Was that Fate's great joke: to come full circle to our beginnings like salmon swimming upstream?

The sky darkened, but there was no sign of impending rain. Another precious two hours passed as Thaddeus wandered among the dead. A strong odour of damp grass and decay wafted about him. The scent was neither pleasant nor unpleasant. It welcomed and repelled him. "Where are you?" he whispered into the silence. "Mom, Dad, Auntie Annie?"

He was suddenly seized with terror at being alone in this eerie place two weeks before Christmas. He could just see the gate of the cemetery in the distance. He turned slowly, casting his eyes across the graveyard.

A few feet away, he heard rustling amongst the fallen leaves. He froze. Turning his whole body slowly and carefully in the direction of the sound, his eyes fell upon three shapes delicately shrouded in the mist descending overhead.

***

From where he stood, he could barely make out three small figures dressed in black coats. Notwithstanding his trepidation and a sudden sense of fear, he moved closer to them and saw a young girl and two little boys. *The Holy Trinity waits to take you, Thaddeus.* The observation made him smile.

The girl held a huge bunch of handpicked flowers in her hand. One little boy was bent over, wiping the face of the small gravestone with his sleeve. The smaller of the two boys stood rigid with one hand in his pocket and the other holding tight to the hand of the girl. Thaddeus didn't want to startle them, he being the only other person in the Necropolis. The huge wreath and two dozen lilies he had carried for hours had made his arms numb, and he yearned to find his family graves to put them down.

"Good afternoon," he said softly to the Holy Trinity as he approached.

The two boys looked suspiciously at him, but the girl smiled. "Hello."

"It's getting late to be in here," said Thaddeus as he looked at his watch. He was suddenly aware of the danger that might befall three angels as the late afternoon darkness of a Glasgow winter descended.

"We've come to put flowers on our Granny's grave," replied the little girl. Her face was earnest, yet it bore the expression of a gentleness of spirit far beyond her years.

"You're no from 'round here," observed the older boy. The thick Glaswegian accent contrasted with the young face and made Thaddeus smile.

"No, I'm from Canada."

The little girl's eyes were wide. "And you're here all by yourself?" she whispered in disbelief. "Will you be alone at Christmas?"

"No, dear," replied Thaddeus. He stifled a smile at her genuine concern, for to do so might offend her and place her sympathy in the realm of the childish. "I'm staying with an old friend in Stirling."

"Oh, that's lovely," she replied with relief. "It must be terrible for folk to be alone at Christmas."

"That's an awful grand load of flowers you've got there, mister," remarked the older boy.

"They're for my parents and relatives," replied Thaddeus.

"You're an orphan?" The little girl was aghast.

"Yes, I suppose I am." Thaddeus hardly thought of being an orphan at fifty-one years of age. Orphans conjured up images of Dickensian children slaving over treadmills in their bare feet.

"What's your name?" asked the smallest boy, wiping his nose on his sleeve.

"Davey, stop that," ordered the little girl, handing him a used tissue.

"Thaddeus," he replied.

"Tad—what?" asked the boy.

"Thaddeus," he repeated slowly and clearly.

"That's a real posh name," observed the older boy.

"It's a silly name," agreed Thaddeus, smiling. "And you are?" Thaddeus asked the girl.

"Mary—Mary McVittie, and this is my brother Bobby and my younger brother Davey."

Thaddeus fixed his eyes on Mary. Where had he seen that face before? She was an exquisite child. Her thick wavy hair framed a perfect milk-white face, out of which large blue-green eyes stared at him. The delicate pink of her cheeks and those of her brothers looked as if they had been airbrushed onto the porcelain skin. He witnessed another masterpiece of the Almighty in the haunting beauty of these three children.

Why did she look so familiar? Thaddeus traced the outlines of his memory, casting far back to faces now forgotten or dead. As Mary laid the flowers on her granny's grave and the Trinity bowed their heads in prayer, he remembered his father's closest sister Annie. There was an old picture in the family album of her when she was around the same age as Mary. The two girls were almost identical.

The unseen hand rested gently on Thaddeus' shoulder, moving him along to the row of graves behind the children. A thin ray of light caught a marble stone, and there before his eyes were the words *James and Margaret Dunvegin*. Tears welled up in his eyes as he placed the wreath over the cold stone. "I'll join you soon," he murmured. While trudging through the Necropolis all afternoon, hadn't he passed this row of graves? Why had he found it just now?

He laid the lilies on the old stone marker of his grandparents and his father's siblings. The two plots were side by side, but Thaddeus could barely read the names. His eyes were blinded by the well of tears rising and impeding his vision. He threw his head heavenward to force the tears back, watching the grey clouds close in. It was after three but already darkness was fast descending.

He thought of the Trinity, now arranging flowers in the two little urns on either side of the stone. They couldn't walk home in this darkness, not in this part of Glasgow. He approached Mary and offered them a ride in a taxi.

"We're no supposed to take rides from strangers," said Bobby.

Thaddeus gave the children his most heartfelt assurances that he meant no harm. "After all, there will be three of you and the driver, and one of me."

Little Davey was all set to risk his own safety just to ride in a shiny black car.

Sheltered by the warmth of innocence and impelled by the unseen hand, Thaddeus set off with the Holy Trinity through the cold and enveloping Glasgow fog.

***

Mary invited Thaddeus to join the family for supper, but he politely refused. The last thing Mrs. McVittie needed was a stranger to feed at this time of year. The black stone tenement building glowing in the streetlights from the recent rain shouted *opportunity needed*. For that to make an appearance, money was required.

Through the half-open curtains at one of the windows, a woman looked down. She threw open the sash and called in a gentle voice to the children.

"Are you sure you won't come in?" asked Mary again.

"No, dear, but thank you. By the way, which flat is yours?"

"Number five—up there. We're coming, Ma."

Thaddeus took note of the address. "Oh Mary, there's something I forgot to ask."

"What?"

"Where do you go to school?"

She told him and then added, "Da says as soon as I reach working age, I'm to get a job in a shop. I want to work at the Stockwell China Bazaar; all those beautiful tea sets and china figurines!"

Thaddeus was crushed. The desire for fine possessions would blind her to every other ambition she might have pursued.

"Mary," Thaddeus began.

"Yes?"

"If you didn't have to work, what would you like to do?"

"Oh, I'd become a teacher."

For a moment, there was a hint of regret behind the wide eyes. She understood that her options would expire worthless. Maturity had already resigned her to a life controlled by that economic class into which she had been born.

***

He was in the car now, taking the back roads to Stirling, and considering the decisions he'd made these past few days. Without conducting extensive research into his investment, he had bequeathed a considerable fortune in his will to Mary McVittie, a nine-year-old girl he met once in a graveyard. He threw his head back and laughed. Of course, he couldn't forget her brothers, so they, too, would receive handsome sums toward their education.

He didn't care much about the boys, but Mary would be his posthumous project. He had visited her school, and as he expected, she was an excellent student. Her academic strengths lay in English, history, and composition. But what did he really know of her or her family? Her teachers informed him that she was a girl who showed promise and who would be laid waste by poverty. Thaddeus would have none of that. Why couldn't she be permitted a solid education? Why shouldn't she be the child he sought? What difference did it make if he selected her as the one beneficiary he could put a face to? The unseen hand had led him to her, amongst the voices of the dead and in the presence of his late parents. The deed was done and dusted. There was nothing more to ponder in the matter of Mary McVittie.

"Have you lost your mind?" Alastair's voice was shrill on the other end of the line. "You met them in a graveyard, you dropped them off at home, and you'll never see them again. The father could be a criminal, and they could be little con artists in training!"

"They're good people," Thaddeus replied. "When I'm gone and the money in that trust is distributed, it will be directed according to the academic achievement of the recipients. But what kind of youth will get these scholarships? They could grow up to become dictators funded through my trust. I won't know a thing about them personally—what they look like, how they speak, whether they're compassionate human beings."

"And this Mary McVittie fits the bill? What about investigating before you invest?" Alastair was nearly shouting on the other end of the line.

"I make my living based on sudden decisions that are informed by my perception of human behaviour. I'm an artist at reading people. I know when they're greedy and I know when they're scared. I don't need to labour over a thing for days to know what's right. Yes, Mary McVittie fits the bill. Enough said." He put down the phone before Alastair could reply.

A winter sun shrouded in light fog beamed overhead, lighting the road to Stirling. The air smelled fresh and sweet. Wreaths hung from the little houses he passed. He saw it all for the last time. He thought of Mary and the little Hummel figurine called *Busy Student* that he had sent her for Christmas. In the card, he wrote "You'll make a great teacher," and used Stirling as the return address. In the New Year, Alastair would contact her family about the legacy, but her gift to Thaddeus was the greater treasure: she connected with him. There was something surreal about her face, her hair, her gentle manner that had touched his soul.

While navigating the umpteenth roundabout in another ancient village, the quality she possessed came to him. She was all children— the one he had been, and the ones he would never meet—and Destiny had brought them together.

***

Thaddeus spent the last year of his life in northern Scotland. The loneliness and majesty of the sweeping hills, coupled with the roaring waves beating against the outermost shores, were a soul mate for his solitude. In the deepest recesses of his heart, he identified with the isolation and became a kindred spirit with nature. He passed his days walking through the rough beauty of the stone-encrusted hills. He didn't write a single option, but he did write to Mary. She had sent a Christmas card to his friend's home in Stirling, and he had replied with a long letter about the trip he would be taking through Scotland. On two occasions, he ventured down to Glasgow to take her to the Willow Tearooms on Sauchiehall Street. There, he watched with unadulterated pleasure as she devoured her favourite treat of high tea. He didn't mention his illness; she would find out soon enough.

His old school friend in Stirling, who had become a doctor, supplied him with sufficient drugs to see out the end of his days. Often in the last few months of his life, he drove out to Dunnet Head from his cottage overlooking the sea and contemplated what it would be like to simply vanish from the end of the earth. When the pain overtook his liberal intake of morphine, he fantasized about a quick and dramatic end. Even as a lapsed Catholic, he couldn't do it. Was God an option? If so, what price would he pay for this unbearable time decay?

In the end, he was found in his cottage by a postman who had tried to push a large envelope from Mary through the letterbox, but something impeded it on the other side. He had gone around to the back door to call and, finding it open, went in to have a look. Thaddeus lay in a heap by the front door. There was no drama, no fanfare. The authorities contacted his friend in Stirling and arrangements were made for his burial in the Necropolis. A careful man, Thaddeus had left a letter of instruction, complete with contact names and numbers, for his disposal (his words).

***

Every year on the anniversary of the day they met, Mary McVittie placed a hand-picked posy of flowers on Thaddeus' grave. Her brothers always had other commitments, and boys being boys, the tradition of remembering their benefactor wasn't top of mind.

"He changed our lives," Mary would remonstrate.

The answer was always the same. "And he didn't seem the type who wanted a lot of fuss made of it."

It was Mary McVittie, professor of English Literature at the University of Glasgow, and the one recipient of his vast wealth who remembered him with tears and flowers and genuine friendship. On each of the three times they had met, her eyes peered into his soul. She was sincere, unaffected, and unsullied by the harshness of the world. She drew him into her with her tenderness and childlike enjoyment of simple pleasures. It was a fitting tribute from the one person with whom he had finally made a profound and lasting connection.

PEANUT BUTTER AND PICKLES
JANET DOLEMAN

This fictional piece was inspired by our first trip to the Bahamas and several things that intrigued me: the impossibly aqua-coloured sea, the colourful culture at the marketplace, the widespread devastation that is still evident years after violent hurricanes hit the islands. The fictional woman at the centre of the story is a composite character, inspired by conversations with people we met on the cruise ship, the ferry, or in church on Easter Sunday in Freeport.

Marion reached into the lower cupboard and took out the large plastic peanut butter jar, cradling its heaviness in the crook of her arm. She stood up slowly, taking a moment to survey the room and the productivity of an afternoon's—actually, a whole winter's—work.

It was time. Now that the four commissioned paintings were sold, wrapped, and ready for delivery, it was time for her to pack up and leave Grand Bahama Island. Tomorrow, the paintings were being picked up by the shipper. Her refrigerator shelves were mostly bare, and the grocery cupboard depleted. Josefina would arrive in her battered blue minivan taxi for the trip to the airport, her dark skin gleaming and her signature closely cropped blond hair and wide smile perpetually in place. Josefina had a habit of talking the whole way, her right arm resting on the open window ledge while steering with her left (a remnant of the island's British past), ready to wave and call greetings to everyone she knew, which was, literally, everyone she saw.

If it hadn't been for Josefina and her friends at the complex, Marion mused, she might not have considered returning to the island after Edward's death ten years before. That almost did her in, sapping her spirit and her energy to make the annual trek from their home in Massachusetts to the sun-baked strip of coral and rock where she and Edward had wintered for thirty years.

Thirty-nine and counting—nine of those on her own, she corrected, with a small sense of pride. Independence was hard won and reluctantly accepted. Edward wasn't coming back, and she might as well get on with living.

Technically, Edward was still with her, tucked away silently in the peanut butter jar that she kept under the buffet in the dining room. At least, some of him was, just as he'd requested. Marion let her mind drift back to that day in the hospital room after the doctors had been in and gone again and the two of them were left alone. They'd clasped hands on the pale blanket draped over Edward's bony knees.

"Well," he'd said. "I guess that's that." He'd sighed deeply, looked at her sadly at first, then gripped her hand tightly and said, cheerily, "Just put me in an old peanut butter jar and take me to the island. Then I know that I can watch those brilliant sunsets with you from the verandah."

Edward had loved the island. Thirty years. He never tired of the long trip, the tedious customs line-ups, the packing and unpacking. It was a grand adventure and a welcome respite from the damp chill of northeast U.S. winters, the relentless wind and icy rain. After one severe winter storm, when they'd lost a row of fruit trees to the ice, Edward suggested selling the farm, moving to an apartment and spending part of each winter "somewhere south, where it was warm." Once they'd found this piece of paradise and settled in, he'd claimed it, puttering about the yard and launching his small boat into the aqua-hued water to go fishing. They became friends with the next-door neighbours who also returned year after year, establishing a connection that grew into a comfortable community. Once Edward retired, they extended their winter sojourn to four or five months, and each trip was like coming home.

Marion was glad Edward hadn't been around to witness the damage from two Category 3 hurricanes that had pummelled the island in 2004, followed by *Wilma* the following year. One hotel was so extensively damaged, the rumour was that the owners merely collected the insurance money and fled the island, abandoning the building as a sad eyesore sticking up out of the flat landscape, windowless openings patched with water-stained plywood. The parking lot deteriorated into a desolate wasteland of cracked cement, overgrown weeds, and bits of broken glass. The International Bazaar nearby took on an air of neglect, its brightly painted buildings now faded and pockmarked after being scoured by salt and sand driven by those terrifying winds. Only a few shopkeepers had returned, halfheartedly draping colourful cotton wraps over gaping holes. Most tourists shopped now at the Port Lucaya Marketplace, closer to the new Casino Hotel.

Edward would have been heartsick, especially with the destruction at their townhouse complex. Marion remembered the telephone call from Josefina, informing her of the extent of the damage. The two back-to-back hurricanes, *Frances* and *Jeanne*, had created a huge mess in the complex, destroying a wall between two units, soaking the furniture, scattering debris from tattered and twisted palmettos and from the beach. By the time Marion and her son and daughter arrived on the island to assess the damage and begin the cleanup, there was little left to salvage. They shovelled and swept and mopped and lugged out sodden couches and mattresses, spraying disinfectant to combat the smell of rotting vegetation and dead animals. Josefina and her large family offered temporary shelter until they could get repairs made and the house livable once again.

Over the last nine years, my painting has improved to where I'm working with a vengeance, Marion mused. *I'm producing better paintings than ever and am gaining a wider client base. The house is cool and comfortable, just the way I like it. I have good friends and neighbours nearby, and to top it all off, Edward and I watch the sunsets together almost every night. Edward's death and the storm damage were a turning point in my life, just like the births of our children, but time is marching on and so am I.*

Which reminded her, it was time. Not only time to leave the island to enjoy the New England summer and fall months, but time for their date. Part of Edward was here with her, and the rest of him was in a matching jar in her apartment back in Springfield, hidden away in her bedroom closet. She didn't think he would mind. He'd gotten his wish to spend his days on the island although he'd had to wait in a big glass pickle jar for a month until she had eaten all the peanut butter.

He'd get a kick out of that, she thought, being pickled. She cradled the plastic container in her arms and carried it out to the verandah, settling into her favourite chair, facing west.

EXHALE
PAUL BOURGEOIS

We, ourselves, are just momentary organizations of chaos, our minds organizing that chaos into patterns.

"**B**reathe in. Breathe in the Universe. Feel the breath, let the vital spirit fill you from the top of your head to the tip of your fingers. Hold it. Hold it inside you. This is Life. And now. Exhale."

The gong indicated the end of the meditation session. Slowly, Thomas Black opened his eyes and extended his arms to his sides, mandala over his head, representing the temporary illusion of this life contained by the eternal circle of birth and death and chaos on the outside. He reached underneath him and pulled out the pillow on which he sat cross-legged and moved to return it to the pile of pillows in the corner of the gymnasium.

"Gong."

Incense permeated the room. All around him, the others seemed to be waking as if from a dream. He really needed these sessions every Monday and Friday afternoon, especially after the stress of the accident.

"Gong."

He grabbed his jacket from the chair. Marilyn Fox was alone near the door, putting on her coat. She had blond curly hair, a beautiful face but with a slight twist in her smile on the right side. Somehow it made her look gentle so he wasn't afraid of her. He had been getting to know her for weeks now but had, up to now, been unable to ask her out.

"Gong."

"Nice time," he said, sidling up to her. "I could really get into it today. Nice to leave the week behind."

"Yeah," she laughed, pulling her collar up and brushing her hair out from underneath, shaking it free. "I've been having some trouble letting go."

"Do you have some time? Do you want to go out for a coffee or something? Maybe I could give you some pointers."

She looked at him and thought for a moment. "Okay," she smiled.

He walked her out and they stood under the ying-yang poster of the meditation group.

"Where do you want to go?" Thomas asked.

"I don't know this area very well. But I am kind of hungry."

"There's an Indian food place around the corner. How do you feel about that?"

"Oh, I like it hot."

It was his turn to pause.

She laughed. "No, not like that. I spent six months in India working in a Gandhian Ashram. We built a well and taught the farmers. The food was hot."

He breathed out. "Oh. Well then, you could probably give me some pointers about meditation."

"Maybe," she laughed.

"This way," he said and started down the street. She followed him.

"You are the nervous type," she observed.

"I'm sorry," he said.

She laughed again.

They ordered extra hot tandoori chicken and chapatis. He ordered a Coke. She had an Indian chai. A young, thin Indian girl, very dark, in a tight sari brought out the chapatis, some hot chutney, and drinks to begin.

"Try the tea," she encouraged while they waited for the food. He sipped his tea. She watched, moving from his eyes to his lips and back.

"Mmm, very nice," he said. "So I guess there's not much I can tell you about this meditation stuff."

"Why, because I spent some time in India? It's not about where you come from," she explained. "It all has to do with the individual. Like me. I'm the nervous fidgety type. I just can't relax."

"You seem pretty relaxed to me."

"You should see me without the meditation sessions. I'm like a mother hen."

"Are—are you?"

"Am I what?"

"A mother?"

"No."

"Oh."

"Why would you ask such a thing? Do I look like a mother?"

175

"I—but—you said—" Speechless, he dipped his bread in the chutney and stuffed it in his mouth. It was so hot, tears came to his eyes. She watched him sweat.

"I don't have any children. I'm single," she told him finally.

"Oh," he answered.

"The Buddhists say this life is an illusion," she explained, changing the subject. "A chaotic creation of the mind, a kind of test for the world we will pass into after we die."

"This life is only a test for the next world. It sounds very Catholic to me."

"I don't think much of religion," she answered him. "I go there mostly for the relaxation techniques. Why do you meditate?"

He paused. "I—I had an accident," he said.

The young girl came with the food. He could smell her slight perfume amidst the curry, light and refreshing. She set a huge red naked chicken and two plates between them. They ate in awkward silence for the rest of the evening.

***

"I had a nice time," she told him outside the restaurant, pulling her coat on and shaking her hair free. "I'm driving uptown."

"I catch a bus downtown," he explained.

"You want a lift?"

He paused again, but only an instant. "Sure."

***

After she returns him home, he strips and lies in bed staring at the ceiling. It is hot. Traffic in the street outside causes moving shadows across the ceiling. Slowly, he drifts off to sleep. Even though he can't remember—the car had hit him from behind as he crossed the street—he always dreams of the accident.

One dream he has is this. It is all a white mist. He is traveling in a coach or a train with others. There is no feeling of fear but a feeling of great warmth and comfort, something otherworldly about the place he finds himself. The vehicle stops in the middle of the road. He gets out and stands in front of the vehicle, spreading his arms to his sides like a human sacrifice. He can see the passengers inside the car, looking out at him. The car starts up again and hits him hard. He is almost grateful.

He awakens in a sweat and is unable to sleep afterwards.

"Release. Release this state of confusion, this world. Exhale."

"Gong."

This time, they went to a Middle Eastern restaurant and had falafels.

The table was lit by candles and the light made her hair golden. "Do you want to tell me about your accident?" she asked him.

"There's not much to tell," he told her. "I don't remember it. I was unconscious for three weeks. I had strange dreams and awoke in the hospital. Everything had changed. I still haven't... I was going to work on a motorcycle with a friend. I used to drive motorcycles. A beautiful Harley, you know, the kind in *Easy Rider*. I had bought a small can of motor oil and was crossing the street... and... and..."

She could see he was becoming agitated. "When there is something someone can't accept," she said, changing the subject, "sometimes people get trapped between worlds. They kind of cycle on the same event they can't handle over and over again, and they can't move on. Sometimes they need a guide." She glowed in the candlelight.

"What are you trying to say?"

"Well, that's what this meditation is for, isn't it, to help you discard the illusions of the mind, desires, expectations, fears..."

They had Baklava for dessert. It was so sweet it made him lightheaded. She drove him home again to the front door of his rundown apartment building.

"Do you want to come up for a bit?" he asked shyly.

"I would love to," she said, "but I can't. I have to work tomorrow."

"Oh, I see," he answered, starting to open the car door.

"What about Friday?" she asked. "I don't work on Saturday."

"Okay."

***

In his dream, he is flying, floating above his bed in the hospital. And then he is traveling through the corridors, searching for something. He is late for an appointment.

He wakes, gasping for breath, his heart pounding in his chest.

***

"Nothing exists. Even you are an illusion. Let go of all illusions. Exhale."

He took her to his apartment on Friday afternoon. It was a one-bedroom with a tiny balcony, the living room full of bookcases piled with books, ones that he could no longer read as if the pages had become blank.

He took her coat, touching her neck and shoulders, and hung it in the closet. She sat down in his own big armchair which faced the window and the big screen TV.

"Do you have anything to drink?" she asked.

"Some red wine," he said, looking in the kitchen cupboard above the broom closet and bringing down a bottle.

"Fine, thanks."

On the table was a little book in red leather. She picked it up and opened it. It was a hundred-year-old copy of *The Rubaiyat of Omar Khayyam*.

"I know this book," she said. "He was a mathematician and an engineer. As he neared the end of his life, he wondered what was beyond, but being a practical logical man with a foundation in science, he couldn't give into blind belief. He says we should drink the wine of life, seize love because this is the world we know, and we cannot know what is beyond, if there is anything beyond. But you know, in his poetry, wine is life and the tavern is the world. Woe to the person who takes everything literally, who cannot read metaphor. If a person could see the truth, they might see that there is nothing beyond. Everything is already here."

Thomas brought the bottle and two full wine glasses, and set them down on the small table beside her. He lit a candle.

She looked at the wine bottle and then at him quizzically. "It's Manischewitz."

"Yeah? So?"

"Well, that's a kosher wine. And it's Friday."

"It was the cheapest I could find."

"Well, I suppose we should say a blessing, you know, just to be respectful. Blessed are You, Master of the universe, who gives us the fruit of the vine, I think it goes. L'chaim." She lifted the glass and drank.

He knelt at her feet, reached across her to his glass on the table and drank it empty. He was nervous. She smiled and refilled his glass.

"You know, for someone who doesn't think much of religion, you certainly know a lot about the stuff," he said.

"Religion is for people," she explained. "But it's my job to know these things."

"I don't understand."

"You're cute," she smiled, rubbing her fingers through his hair.

His body responded. It had been so long since the accident, since he had lost everything. He didn't understand and he didn't want to. He touched her hand in his hair then ran his fingers down her arm to her shoulder and then to her cheek. Then he kissed her.

And she kissed him back.

As the evening progressed, they drank the rest of the wine. Their clothes were scattered throughout the apartment. She lay on top of him. The streetlight was especially bright, shining on the ceiling. The shadows and shapes were soft. He stared up at her as her golden hair hung down and brushed his chest.

"I suppose you want to know what's going on," she said. It wasn't the light from the street shining on the ceiling. It was her.

"Yes."

"Don't be afraid," she said, stroking his cheek.

"No," he answered.

There was only her in the room. In fact, there was no room. Bathed in her light, he didn't know if even he existed.

"You didn't survive the accident."

He didn't even know if she was there. There was only light.

"Exhale."

ABOUT THE AUTHORS

Paul Bourgeois –

Paul has a BA in English literature, a BFA in Fine Arts, and a Masters degree in Library Sciences. He has lived in India, Nepal, Japan, Vietnam, the Czech Republic, and Finland. He has written for newspaper and radio, produced short films and documentaries, had various poems and stories published. He has worked with computer animation and is currently developing a graphic novel.

Janet Doleman –

Janet grew up in the small community of Barrington Passage on Nova Scotia's South Shore. She remembers her grandmother's original poems in birthday cards, which inspired her to write. She carries on a family tradition of writing diaries, letters and journals. Janet earned her B.A. in English and a University diploma in Secretarial Science at Acadia University, Wolfville, NS, and lives in Dartmouth with husband George. Their daughter Katie lives and works nearby; son Michael works in law enforcement in British Columbia.

Janet's publications are as follows:

Tidings, publication of the United Baptist Woman's Missionary Union of the Atlantic Provinces, March 2016 issue, p. 19 'Easter Hats' in the 'Tell the Story' column.

LEGION magazine, January/February 2015 issue, pp.27-29, 'Lines from the Front, Three Letters From Three Wars.'

Gazette, Dartmouth Heritage Museum Society, June 2014 issue, p. 4, 'Nova Scotia Writers, Part II' or 'Strange Sightings, Songs and Soul-Baring Underground' (about the Evergreen Writers' Group).

Maida Barton Follini –

Maida is a Connecticut Yankee transplanted to Nova Scotia in 1980. Her interests include Genealogy and History, and she edits a Family Newsletter circulated to over 100 kinfolk. While living in Amherst, Nova Scotia, Maida wrote a series on the history of churches in Cumberland County, and a monthly column for the Amherst Daily News. Her poem, "Osprey's Call" won the Cumberland County Library's poetry writing contest, and she has had several poems published in journals of the Religious Society of Friends (Quakers). Moving to Dartmouth, N.S. in 2008, Maida volunteers at the Dartmouth Heritage Museum, where she edits the Museum *Gazette*. She has authored the museum pamphlet "A Quaker Odyssey: The Migration of Quaker Whalers from Nantucket, Massachusetts to Dartmouth Nova Scotia and Milford Haven, Wales."

John Gabriel –

John was born in Dublin. As a young man he traveled extensively and eventually settled in Canada. The love of Celtic music and the wilderness became a huge part of his life. He traveled as a single entertainer for a number of years on the music circuit in Canada and the U.S. doing gigs and enjoying what he loved best. Later, he tired of the night life and settled into the forest world as a woodsman. He has written seven books, all nonfiction but for one—*The Apprentice Doryman*. All books are available on Amazon Kindle in e-book form: *A Life Almost Wasted, A Waste of a Human Being, The Crucifixion of Palestine, Growing Up in Dublin, Paranormal, Cannabis Oil Cured My Cancer*, and *The Apprentice Doryman*. The books *Cannabis Oil Cured My Cancer* and *A Life Almost Wasted* are available in paperback on Amazon. John now resides in Halifax, Nova Scotia, Canada.

Frank Leaman –

Frank has worked in media developing stories for a cable TV station in Bridgewater. Frank has also written articles for community newspapers. Frank has written a book, *The Roar of the Sea*, about his grandfather's seafaring experience. Frank is a member of the Evergreen Writers Group and enjoys learning from other likeminded folk. Frank's story about a journey from Puerto Rico to Nova Scotia has, as well as fiction, some truth inspired by his paternal grandfather who came to Canada.

Frank has had a varied career. He has worked in tourism, cable TV, land development, salvage, lumbering, and antique sales.

Catherine A. MacKenzie –

Cathy escapes from her mundane world by writing poems and short fiction most women can relate to. Although she writes all genres, she enjoys veering toward the dark. She has been published in print and online publications. She has also self-published several short story collections, books of poetry, and children's picture books.

Cathy lives with her husband in Halifax, Nova Scotia. She winters in Ajijic, Mexico, where her works have appeared in local publications. Her amazing, gorgeous grandchildren provide much of her joy and inspiration. Cathy's website: **www.writingwicket.wordpress.com**

Janet McGinity –

Janet was born in Moncton, New Brunswick to an Acadian mother and a father of Irish descendant, and is fluently bilingual. She has been telling or writing stories all her life, and counts getting her first library card at age seven as among the most important events of her life. She worked as a staff writer with the Telegraph-Journal in Saint John, New Brunswick in the 1980s, and has also worked in radio and published a few magazine articles.

She lives in Halifax, where after leaving journalism, she worked for the federal government for many years. Now happily retired, Janet has time and freedom to devote to writing. She is currently working on a historical novel set in Jersey, Channel Islands, and Isle Madame, Cape Breton, along with shorter works. She is one of the founding members of Evergreen Writers Group.

Elizabeth McGinley –

Elizabeth studied English literature and philosophy, graduating with an Honours BA from Carleton University. She worked for many years as a consulting business analyst and writer in the Information Technology industry for governments and private corporations. To paraphrase Winston Churchill, she now makes a living writing options, and makes a life writing fiction. She has travelled extensively and now lives in Nova Scotia.

Judi Risser –

Judi expresses what inspires, moves and elevates her through both her writing and her photography. Her source of inspiration comes from all types of sense perceptions experienced in her connection with the inherent beauty in the universe's endless gifts. Her sources are endless... Emotion, experience and expression vary on so many levels, depth and comprehension. She can't ever imagine a life without her camera or her notes pages on her phone, her electronic scribbler.

Influenced from more than 20 years in the Canadian Military, in both the Medical and Education Training and Development Occupations, Judi believes that it is our inherent responsibility to share experiences, strength and hope as it helps us recognize ourselves in others...minimizing perceived gaps in all areas of human existence...bringing us closer to each other, ultimately, to reality.

Additionally, Judi was honoured when her images of well loved places from her childhood at Risser's Beach and across the Bay in

Petite Riviere, were chosen as the front and back covers of the Evergreen Writers Group, Journeys Anthology.

Judi is a member of the highly acclaimed Lunenburg Art Gallery where she enjoys showing her locally inspired art work and meeting tourists from all over the world when volunteering as Curator.

For more on what Judi is up to, please visit both of her websites. They are as diverse as are her interests and creative expression.

Judi's Fine Art Black and White Photography site:
https://soulsearching.live

Judi's Poetry and Soulful Spaces and Special Places Blog:
https://weareallawakening.wordpress.com

Tom Robson –

Tom started to write in his forties when his target audiences were the elementary students he taught. Flushed with two successes in Atlantic writing contests, he continued this into retirement. Writing was a hobby, purely for enjoyment, until he had three ghost stories published in *Out of the Mist*, an anthology compiled by the Evergreen Writers Group. His adaptation into a performance piece of Catherine Scholes' book *Peace Begins with You* is in *The Peaceful School: Models That Work* by Hetty Van Gurp.

A collection of stories and poems, some true, some depending on artistic licence and selective memory, were written over a thirty-year period. They have been assembled into *Written While I Still Remember: A Patchwork Memoir,* published in 2014 by Mackenzie Publishing.

Tom enjoys writing short stories and journals of his travels. He occasionally tries to be poetic. He wants to gather his poems from the depths of his computer memory for publication. This will have to wait until he proves that it is possible for a man in his eightieth year to write a successful romantic novel.

Tom was born a proud Yorkshireman and enjoyed his youth in the New Forest where he first became a teacher. He came to Canada in 1971. He now lives with his wife in Halifax, Nova Scotia.

Visit Tom's website: **https://robsonswritings.wordpress.com.**

Art White –

In the dedicatory remarks of his book, Art writes: "To my father, a letter-writing man, in whose likeness I'm proud to be compared." Also on that page was this: "To Henry Cowan, my boyhood English teacher, who valued a well-turned phrase above one purfectly spelt."

In the lee of those mentors, as a manuscript preacher, story-teller/writer, author and playwright, Mr. White has well-turned phrases all his life. His CV includes more than 200 magazine stories and articles in the United States and Canada, a collected work: "From Away, Here to Stay" and, in recent years, dozens of plays and historical readings, in which he has occupied roles as producer, director, actor, publicist and ticket-taker.

Wilma Stewart-White –

Always a voracious reader from early days, she is also a journal keeper so the step into writing was natural.

A retired business owner and museum curator she is also an avid gardener and traveler.

Her teacher training left her with a healthy respect for grammar and spelling and a deep love of books especially biographies and English novels.

In retirement, she and her husband live in Dartmouth in the winter and at the family cottage in Indian Point in the summer where she enjoys family visits from her eight grandchildren. Spring and fall are her travelling months

She has published two histories of Mahone Bay and has in the works several short stories about her travels and a mystery set in Mahone Bay where she lived for 30 years.

Phil Yeats –

Phil is a retired scientist experimenting with creative writing. He has a keen interest in environmental science and dabbled in yachting and golf before turning to fiction. Phil is the author of nine published short stories and one poem. Several of these were written using the pen name Alan Kemister to keep a minimal separation between his real science and the fictional variants in the stories. He is working on a series of mystery novels about a detective in a fictional town on Nova Scotia's South Shore. More information about these writing projects is available at **https://alkemi47.blogspot.com.**

ABOUT LESLEY CHOYCE

Lesley Choyce is a novelist and poet living at Lawrencetown Beach, Nova Scotia. He is the author of 84 books for adults, teens and children. He teaches in the English Department and Transition Year Program at Dalhousie University. He is a year-round surfer and founding member of the 1990s spoken word rock band, The SurfPoets. Choyce also runs Pottersfield Press, a small literary publishing house and hosted the national TV show, Off The Page, for many years. His books have been translated into Spanish, French, German and Danish and he has been awarded the Dartmouth Book Award and the Ann Connor Brimer Award.

https://www.lesleychoyce.com/

LINKS AND SOCIAL MEDIA

Evergreen Writers Group Website:
www.evergreenwritersgroup.wordpress.com

***

Visit us on Facebook:

Evergreen Writers Group (page)
https://www.facebook.com/evergreenwritersgroup/

Evergreen Writers Group (public group)
https://www.facebook.com/groups/410713765644039/

Off Highway (book page)
https://www.facebook.com/EvergreenWritersJourneys/

Out of the Mist (book page)
https://www.facebook.com/EvergreenWritersGhostAnthology/

***

OUT OF THE MIST: 22 Atlantic Canadian Ghost Stories
(Evergreen's first anthology, published 2014)

Available at Amazon
(print and e-book)

Made in the USA
Lexington, KY
15 July 2018